MARBLES

IDENTIFICATION AND PRICE GUIDE

REVISED & EXPANDED 4TH EDITION

ROBERT BLOCK

Schiffer Publishing Ltd®

4880 Lower Valley Road, Atglen, PA 19310 USA

Library of Congress Cataloging-in-Publication Data

Block, Robert. 1960-
Marbles : identification and price guide / Robert Block. -- Rev. & expanded 4th ed.
p.   cm.
Includes bibliographical references.
ISBN: 0-7643-1574-9 (pbk.)
1. Marbles (Game objects)--Collectors and collecting--Catalogs.
I. Title.
NK6215.B58   2002
688.7'62--dc21
2002008061
CIP

Revised price guide: 2002
Copyright © 1996, 1998, 1999 & 2002 by Robert Block

ISBN: 0-7643-1574-9
Printed in China
1 2 3 4

Published by Schiffer Publishing Ltd.
4880 Lower Valley Road
Atglen, PA 19310
Phone: (610) 593-1777; Fax: (610) 593-2002
E-mail: Schifferbk@aol.com
Please visit our web site catalog at
www.schifferbooks.com

This book may be purchased from the publisher.
Include $3.95 for shipping. Please try your bookstore first.
We are always looking for people to write books on new and related subjects. If you have an idea for a book please contact us at the above address.
You may write for a free catalog.

In Europe, Schiffer books are distributed by
Bushwood Books
6 Marksbury Avenue
Kew Gardens
Surrey TW9 4JF England
Phone: 44 (0) 20-8392-8585; Fax: 44 (0) 20-8392-9876
E-mail: Bushwd@aol.com
Free postage in the UK. Europe: air mail at cost.

Dedication

This book is dedicated to my parents, Stan and Claire Block, who are the vision and hard work behind the Marble Collectors Society of America; to my sons, Kevin and Benjamin, who represent the next generation of marble players and collectors; and to you, the marble collectors, who have turned a childhood game into a full-fledged hobby.

ACKNOWLEDGEMENTS

No book is written solely by the author. There were a number of other people who contributed in various ways to what you are holding in your hands.

All of the photos in this book are of marbles that have been sold in Block's Box or A Chip Off The Old Block auctions, or are from the collection of Stan and Bob Block. The exception to this is #348, #356, #357, #358, #359, #363, #364, #380 and #391, which are all from the collection of Hansel de Sousa. My thanks to him for sharing these photos.

My thanks to David Tameluvich and Dennis Webb for sharing their research on Alley Agate Company, Heaton Agate Company, JABO Inc., and Cairo Novelty Company.

Several people took the time to proof read the first edition of this book. I would like to thank Harold Sugarman, Jim Palko, Ken Francella and Keith Sibbald for their many valuable and constructive suggestions.

A special thanks to Peter Schiffer and his staff, for their superb support during this project.

Contents

Introduction – 4th Edition

Thank you to everyone who has purchased previous editions of this book. You have made it a huge success. This identification and price guide is consistently ranked by Amazon.com and Barnesandnoble.com as the best-selling marble book. For those of you who are about to enter the wonderful world of marble collecting, you are embarking on a hobby that is rewarding and fun-filled, and sure to restore a little bit of that "kid" to your soul. For those of you who have been collecting for years, I hope this book provides an accurate market guide to you for current market trends.

The hobby of marble collecting continues to experience expansion on a number of fronts.

More and more people are discovering the hobby, as evidenced by the continued growth of membership in the Marble Collectors Society of America and other clubs, and the growth in the number of items offered for sale on the internet and the increasing number of bidders.

We continue to see an overall increase in values, although as with any collectible, some segments show an increase in value and some show a leveling off or even small decrease in value.

The adages "condition is king" and "quality sells while the rest dwells" continue to be true. We have seen Mint examples, graded in the high 9's (out of 10), show marked increases in value when compared to non-Mint examples. This has held true across all segments of the market, regardless of the strength of the particular segment.

The hobby of marble collecting continues to be an active and vibrant community. There are several active bulletin boards on the internet that see spirited discussions throughout the week. Attendance at marble shows has recovered from the dip it took a couple of years ago. The only way to truly learn about marbles is to hold them in your hand and have someone teach you.There is no better place than a marble show to learn about marbles, sit with old friends, and make new ones.

Probably the biggest change we have seen in the three years since I last updated this price guide is the continued rise of the internet as a place to buy and sell marbles. You can find every type and price range of marble for sale on the internet. Unfortunately, an active marketplace breeds charlatans and hucksters. Many fakes and reproductions abound, so you need to be aware. As always, deal with reputable and known dealers and collectors, and always get an unconditional money-back guarantee.

However, don't let these warnings dissuade you from jumping into this wonderful hobby. Out of all the items that I collect, I have to say that you will never meet a more enthusiastic, down-to-earth, helpful and honest group of people, than you do in marble collecting. Play for all the marbles, but remember they are still a child's toy.

Bob Block
Shelton, Connecticut
June, 2002

MARBLE COLLECTORS SOCIETY OF AMERICA

The Marble Collectors Society of America (MCSA) was founded in 1975. The Society is a non-profit organization established for charitable, scientific, literary and educational purposes. It is the oldest and largest marble collecting organization, as well as the only one that is non-profit. The Society's mission is to gather and disseminate information and perform services to further the hobby of marble collecting and the preservation of the history of marbles and marble makers.

In pursuit of this mission, the Society has been engaged in a number of activities for over twenty years. Among the major publications of the Society are the uninter-rupted issuance of a quarterly newsletter *Marble Mania*®, photographing and publish-ing of color identification sheets, compilation of price and identification surveys, pub-lication of several editions of a marble price guide, establishment of a library of articles and marble related material, publication of contributor listings, research and issuance of articles concerning marble factories and contemporary marble makers, and publica-tion of Mark Randall's booklet *Marbles as Historical Artifacts*. The Society has also produced a number of permanent slide presentations on various aspects of marble collecting, a forty-minute videotape on marble making and a two-hour videotape on the basics of marble collecting. Finally, the Society has donated marble collections to several museums including The Smithsonian Institute, The Corning Museum of Glass and the The Wheaton Village Museum.

The future will see continuing research and development of the Society library, additional videotapes in the "A Guide to the Hobby of Marble Collecting" series and the completion of a collection of marbles in sealed cases, which will be available on a loan basis to libraries and museums. For more information about the Society write to Marble Collectors Society of America, P.O. Box 222, Trumbull, CT 06611 or visit: http://www.marblemania.com

VALUATION OF MARBLES

There are four factors that determine the value of a marble: Type, Condition, Size and Eye Appeal.

The most important determinant of marble value is the rarity of the type. Marbles are classified into the following categories:

Handmade Glass (categorized by design)
Cane-cut or Rod-cut
  Swirl
                Latticinio core
                Divided core
                Solid core
                Ribbon core
                Joseph's Coat
                Banded (or coreless)
                Other cores
                Peppermint
                Clambroth
                Banded Opaque
                Indian
                Banded lutz
                Ribbon lutz
                Indian lutz
                Other swirls
  End of Day
                Cloud
                Onionskin
                Panelled onionskin
                Joseph's Coat
                Mist
                Indian
                Banded opaque
                Submarine
                End of day onionskin lutz
                Mist lutz
  Miscellaneous
                Mica
                Slag
                Opaque
                Clearie
  Single-gather
                Sulphide

Cloud
Mica
Paperweight

Handmade Non-Glass

Clay
Bennington
Crockery
Stoneware
China
Carpet ball
Mineral
Agate
Limestone
Other Mineral
Other Material
Wood
Steel
Paper

Machine-Made Marbles (categorized by manufacturer or design)

Manufacturer
Transitional
M.F. Christensen & Son Company
Akro Agate Company
Christensen Agate Company
Peltier Glass Company
Master Marble/Master Glass Company
Vitro Agate Companies
Marble King, Incorporated
Ravenswood Novelty Company
Alley Companies
Heaton Agate Company
Cairo Novelty Company
Champion Agate, Incorporated
Davis Marble Works
Playrite Marble and Novelty Company
Jackon Marble Company
Other manufacturers
Design
Single-stream
Single-color
Slag
Swirl
Variegated-stream or Multiple-stream
Swirl
Corkscrew
Patch
Ribbon

Cat's-eye
Brushed
Veneered
Contemporary Handmade
Artist
Design

When using the price tables in this book, you also have to keep in mind a number of other factors.

Collectors generally size marbles in 1/16″ increments. Unfortunately, we don't have the space in this book to create pricing tables in 1/16″ increments. Therefore, you should use caution and common sense when using these tables. They are average values for the average size within each range in the tables. You should adjust them accordingly for differences in size and condition from the average each table represents.

This book will help you to identify each of these types, and will serve as a guide to their relative rarity. However, rarity is not necessarily an indicator of price. A marble can be so rare that it is unrecognized by most collectors, and have a low price because of low demand. The hobby of marble collecting has also not reached maturity. As a result, the price structure at the high end of the market is still very compressed. The relation between rarity and price is not linear. This means that just because one particular marble is 100 times rarer than another particular type, it is not going to sell for 100 times more. The multiple will tend to be much less.

The second factor that determines the value of a marble is its condition. The grading of condition is very subjective. Every collector has their own opinion and no two collectors will ever agree on the exact condition of a particular marble. The Marble Collectors Society of America uses a descriptive grading system (Mint, Near Mint, Good, Collectible), which allows for some flexibility in grading. A numerical grading system based on a scale of 1 to 10 has also developed among marble collectors. The descriptions of each grading label used by the Society, along with the equivalent numerical grading is:

Mint: A marble that is in original condition. The surface is unmarked and undamaged. There may be some minor rubbing on the surface, however, the marble is just the way it came from the factory. (10.0-9.0)

Near Mint: A marble that has seen minor usage. There may be evidence of some hit marks, usually tiny subsurface moons, pinprick chips, tiny flakes or tiny bruises. The damage is inconsequential and does not detract from viewing the marble. If there is noticeable damage, then it is on only one side of the marble and the other side is Mint. (8.9-8.0)

Good: A marble that has seen usage. It will have numerous hit marks, subsurface moons, chips, flakes or bruises. The core can still be seen clearly, but the marble has obviously been used. If the damage is large or deep, then it is confined to one side and the other side is Mint to Near Mint. (7.9-7.0)

Collectible: A marble that has seen significant usage. Overall moons, chips, flakes and bruises. The core is completely obscured in some spots. A Collectible marble has served its purpose and been well used. Still, it is a placeholder in a collection until a better example comes along. (6.9-0.0)

Any damage to the surface of a marble, no matter how slight, will affect its value. For a given amount of damage, the depreciation of value is much greater for machine-made marbles than for handmade marbles. Even a small chip will effectively reduce the value of a machine-made marble by more than half. Collectors tend to be more forgiving of damage to a handmade marble, probably because handmade marbles are more difficult to find.

The third factor that determines the value of a marble is its size. The size of a marble is measured by its diameter in inches. Marble manufacturers utilized a sieve system of measuring. Using a device that measured marbles in 1/16" increments, the smallest opening that the marble would fall through was the size. Because of this method, the marbles classified as one size by a manufacturer, could in fact vary by 3/64". It was technically almost impossible to produce a handmade glass marble in sizes greater than about 2-1/2" in diameter. The marble would sag and deform during the annealing process because of its weight. However, different types of marbles are more common in some sizes than others. Machine-made marbles are usually 1/2" to 3/4". This is because marble tournament regulations set the size of the shooters to be between 1/2" and 3/4" and the size of the target marbles to be 5/8". Again, the relative rarity of different sizes varies greatly from one type of marble to the next. This guide shows the approximate value by size for each type of marble. You can use this to infer the relative rarity of different marble sizes by marble type.

The final factor that determines the value of a marble is its eye appeal. Eye appeal is related to the brightness of the colors and the symmetry or intricacy of the design. Brightly colored marbles command higher prices. Also, symmetrical or intricate designs tend to command higher prices. Keep in mind that eye appeal is very subjective, more so than condition. Thus, two collectors could value the same marble very differently.

There are no hard and fast rules for determining the value of a marble. You must take each of these four factors into consideration when valuing a marble and bear in mind that the value you decide may be far different from the value that the next collector comes up with.

In this price guide there is a price table provided for each category of marble. The price table shows the approximate price for an average example of a marble within a given size range and for a given condition. These values are derived from Society price surveys, auction results and personal experience. The price tables also show price multiples for variations in a given marble category.

For example, if you had a 1-1/4" latticinio core swirl that was in Mint condition, had a yellow core and was an end of cane marble, then you could calculate the approximate value range as follows:

$80	x	1.10	x	1.25	= $110
value of a		multiple for		low multiple for	
white core	x	yellow core	x	end of cane	= low value

$80	x	1.10	x	2.0	= $175
value of a		multiple for		high multiple for	
white core	x	yellow core	x	for end of cane	= high value

The value for the marble would range between $110 and $175.

Remember that as a marble becomes rarer, the multiples are not completely linear. Just because a marble is 100 times rarer than another does not mean the price of the rare marble is 100 times more than the price of the common one. This is especially true when combining several rarity factors or multiples (for instance, a latticinio core swirl that was both red core and end of cane). Use the multiples only as a guideline.

When using the price tables in this book, you also have to keep in mind a number of other factors. None of the pricing tables discuss buffed and polished marbles. Buffed marbles have some buffing performed on the surface, but the pontils are pretty much intact. Polished marbles are ground more heavily and the pontils are generally missing. When valuing buffed and polished marbles,collectors generally use a value somewhere between the Near Mint and Good columns for handmade marbles and the Good and Collectible columns for machine made marbles.

HANDMADE MARBLES

A handmade marble is a thing of beauty and a technical feat of glasswork and art. While these marbles were made using the "mass production" techniques of the time, in reality each handmade marble is individually crafted by a person. This cannot be said for machine-made marbles. Each handmade marble carries with it the individual stamp of the craftsman who created it. This is in the twist of the marble and in the design and the colors. The appeal of handmade marbles lies in their individuality. No two canes were the same, and no two marbles off the same rod are exactly the same. You cannot say that about most machine-made marbles.

By definition, a handmade marble is a marble that was individually made by a craftsman. Non-glass handmade marbles have existed for almost as long as there have been children. During primitive and medieval times, these were rounded stone or clay marbles and they are not very valuable today. The handmade marbles sought after by today's collectors are those that were produced in Germany during the second half of the 19th century and the first two decades of the 20th century. (Some handmade marbles were produced in the United States during the early 20th century, but these represented a very tiny segment of the market compared to German marbles). German-made glass marbles represented the bulk of the marble market until the early 1920s. The supremacy of German marbles on the playing field finally ended during the early 1900s due to a combination of several factors. These include the American invention of mechanized marble production, the cut-off of German imports into the U.S. during World War I and the Fordney-McCumber Act tariffs of the early 1920s.

All handmade glass marbles have at least one pontil. This is the rough spot at the bottom pole of the marble where it was sheared off its glass cane or a punty.

Handmade marbles are generally classified as either cane-cut (sometimes called rod-cut) or as single-gather. Almost all handmade glass marbles are cane-cut marbles. This type of marble is sheared off the end of a long cane which contains the design of the marble and then is rounded. Single-gather marbles, on the other hand, are produced one at a time on the end of a punty. Handmade marbles can be further classified by the type and/or coloring of the design.

The production of handmade marbles (whether cane-cut or single-gather) was very labor-intensive. For example, the creation of a handmade swirl required between four and twelve separate manual steps. Single-gather marbles could require less steps, but only one marble was produced at a time, rather than a whole set of marbles off of one cane. Suffice to say that the production of handmade marbles was a fairly laborious task. As a result, far less handmade marbles exist than machine-made marbles, therefore increasing their value.

The earliest articles discussing marbles as a collectible were published in the mid-1960s. These articles all dealt with handmade marbles. Early marble collectors, and the hobby is really only about 40 years old, were only interested in handmade marbles. The earliest guide to marble collecting was Morrison and Terrison's *Marbles-Identification and Price Guide*, published in 1968, followed by Baumann's *Collecting Antique Marbles*, published in 1970. Both of these books classified handmade marbles, to almost the complete exclusion of machine-made marbles.

The past decade has seen the handmade segment of the marble market mature. This side of the market has not been experiencing the volatility in price that we have seen in the machine-made side of the market. This does not mean that handmades do not go through price cycles. Different types of handmade marbles go in and out of favor with collectors as their tastes change, but the market has been much less volatile than the machine-made market.

LATTICINIO CORE SWIRLS

Latticinio core swirls are cane-cut marbles. The core consists of strands of colored rods that form a lattice-looking core when the marble is twisted off the cane.

White cores (#1) are the most common, occurring in about 80% of the examples. Yellow cores (#2) occur in about 10% of the examples. Orange cores (#3) and green cores (#4) are rare, occurring in about 2% of the examples. Red cores (#5) or blue cores are the most rare, occurring in very few examples. Alternating strands of two or more different colors (#6, #7) are rare.

Outer layers usually consist of sets of strands or bands. Three-layer (#8) and four-layer examples are also rare. There are very few examples known to exist with completely formed latticinio cores and no outer layer (naked core). Left-hand twist examples are also very rare. Some latticinio core swirls have also been found with some mica flecks in them, but these have been very rare.

Since swirls are cut off the end of a cane, there are first-off-cane and last-off-cane examples. A first-off-cane swirl (#9) usually has the inner design coming right out of the top of the marble. This is because the worker could grasp the full rod of glass and heat the very end of it without using a punty. Last-off-cane swirls (#10) have the inner design going only partly into the marble. The bottom of the marble is usually clear or cloudy glass. This is because the last-off-cane swirl was the nub of the cane that was left over. It was usually attached to a punty with clear glass, resulting in part of the marble not having a design.

You may also find latticinio core swirls that have a base glass that is a color other than clear. Usually, these are amber (#11), blue (#12) or green. These are rare.

#1: White latticinio core swirl

#2: Yellow latticinio core swirl

Latticinio Core Swirls

Size	Mint	Near Mint	Good	Collectible
1/2" or less	12.50	5.00	3.00	1.00
9/16" to 11/16"	12.50	7.00	3.00	1.00
3/4" to 1"	40.00	20.00	7.00	2.00
1" to 1-1/2"	90.00	50.00	25.00	10.00
1-5/8" to 1-7/8"	200.00	125.00	70.00	25.00
2" & over	350.00	175.00	80.00	30.00

These are values for marbles with a white core. Yellow cores have a multiple of 1.10x. Orange or green cores have a multiple of 1.25x to 2x. Red or blue cores have a multiple of 5x to 15x. Marbles with two or more alternating colors in the core have a multiple of 2x to 5x the value of the individual colors. "End-of-cane" marbles have a multiple of 1.5x to 3x. Marbles that have a colored base glass have a multiple of 10x to 20x. Marbles that are in very clear glass or marbles with bright colors have a multiple of 1.5x to 4x.

#3: Orange latticinio core swirl

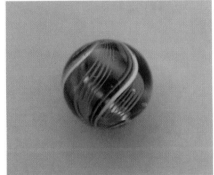

#5: Red latticinio core swirl (in divided form)

#4: Green latticinio core swirl

#6: Alternating latticinio core swirl (red and white core)

#7: Alternating latticinio core swirl (blue and white core)

#10: Last-off-cane latticinio core swirl

#8: Three-layer latticinio core swirl

#11: Amber glass latticinio core swirl

#9: First-off-cane latticinio core swirl

#12: Blue glass latticinio core swirl

DIVIDED CORE SWIRLS

The core of a divided core swirl is formed by three or more separate bands. When the marble is twisted off the cane, the bands form a core with clear spaces in between each band.

The determinants of value of a divided core swirl are the number of inner bands, coloring, quality of workmanship and design. Cores with three or four bands (#13, #14, #15) are the most common. Five-and six-banded cores (#16) are much rarer. The more closely that the outer bands or strands mirror the spaces in the core, the better designed is the marble.

Three-layer (#17) and four-layer examples are rare. Some examples have been found with green aventurine in the inner or outer bands. This is also very rare. There are also some rare "naked" examples with no outer layer (#18).

#13: Four-band divided core swirl

#15: Three-band divided core swirl

#14: Four-band divided core swirl

#16: Six-band divided core swirl

#17: Three-layer divided core swirl

#18: Naked divided core swirl

Divided Core Swirls

Size	Mint	Near Mint	Good	Collectible
1/2" or less	12.50	5.00	3.00	1.00
9/16" to 11/16"	12.50	7.00	3.00	1.00
3/4" to 1"	40.00	20.00	7.00	2.00
1" to 1-1/2"	90.00	50.00	25.00	10.00
1-5/8" to 1-7/8"	200.00	125.00	70.00	25.00
2" & over	350.00	175.00	80.00	30.00

These values are for marbles with three or four bands in the core. Marbles with five or six bands have a multiple of 1.1x to 3x. Marbles with three or more layers have a multiple of 1.5x to 4x. Marbles with aventurine have a multiple of 2x to 6x. "Naked" marbles have a multiple of 1.5x to 5x. Marbles in very clear glass or with bright colors have a multiple of 1.5x.

SOLID CORE SWIRLS

The core of a solid core swirl is formed by bands or strands of color that are placed so closely together that there are no clear spaces in between.

The core can be all the same color, usually white or yellow, or it can be a solid color with colored bands or stripes on it (#19, #20).

Solid core swirls usually have an outer layer of bands or strands. "Naked" solid core swirls (#21), marbles without an outer layer, are rare, but are more common than found in latticinio or divided core swirls. Examples with three or four layers are also rare (#22). Occasionally, the core of the swirl will have three or more lobes (#23). Aventurine has been found in the cores or the outer layers of a few examples. This is rare. Also, some very few examples have been found in colored base glass. This is also very rare.

There are some solid core swirls (as well as latticinio core and divided core) that have very bright colors. These are sometimes referred to by collectors as English-style or Bristol glass (#24), although no evidence has been found that handmade marbles were made in England.

#19: Solid core swirl

#21: Naked solid core swirl

#20: Solid core swirl

#22: Three-layer solid core swirl

#24: English-style solid core swirl

#23: Lobed solid core swirl (view from top)

Solid Core Swirls

Size	Mint	Near Mint	Good	Collectible
1/2" or less	15.00	5.00	3.00	1.00
9/16" to 11/16"	15.00	7.00	3.00	1.00
3/4" to 1"	45.00	22.50	7.00	2.00
1" to 1-1/2"	95.00	55.00	30.00	12.50
1-5/8" to 1-7/8"	210.00	150.00	75.00	30.00
2" & over	375.00	200.00	100.00	60.00

These values are for marbles with single, or two color, white and/or yellow cores. Cores that are more colorful or contain more colors have a multiple of 1.1x to 2x. "Naked" marbles have a multiple of 1.25x to 2x. Marbles with three or more layers have a multiple of 1.25x to 2.5x. Marbles with lobed cores have a multiple of 1.25x to 2.5x. Marbles with aventurine have a multiple of 1.5x to 3x. Marbles with a colored base glass have a multiple of 2. 5x to 10x. Marbles in very clear glass or with bright colors have a multiple of 1.5x.

RIBBON CORE SWIRLS

The core of a ribbon core swirl is a wide, flat band of color in the center of a rod. This band is twisted when the marble is cut off the cane. The degree of twist will vary from flat (no twist) to three or four twists (creating a helix effect).

The core of a ribbon core swirl is usually a solid color with several strands or bands of color on it. It will vary in thickness. The core can consist of one ribbon, which is called a single ribbon (#25, #26), or two ribbons, which is called a double ribbon (#27, #28). Double ribbon core swirls are slightly more common than single ribbon cores.

Ribbon core swirls can either be naked (#29, #30) or have outer bands or strands. Naked ribbon core swirls are slightly rarer than those with outer layers. The outer layer of a ribbon core swirl can mirror the face of the ribbon, or the edge. The better designed and executed the outer layer and ribbon, the more valuable the marble.

#25: Single ribbon core swirl

#27: Double ribbon core swirl

#26: Single ribbon core swirl

#28: Double ribbon core swirl

#29: Naked single ribbon core swirl

#30: Naked double ribbon core swirl

Ribbon Core Swirls

Size	Mint	Near Mint	Good	Collectible
1/2" or less	22.50	15.00	6.00	2.00
9/16" to 11/16"	45.00	25.00	10.00	2.00
3/4" to 1"	150.00	65.00	25.00	10.00
1" to 1-1/2"	250.00	125.00	50.00	25.00
1-5/8" to 1-7/8"	350.00	175.00	80.00	40.00
2" & over	600.00	350.00	150.00	75.00

These values are for marbles with a single ribbon and well-formed outer layers. Double ribbon cores have a multiple of 0.6x to 0.75x. Naked marbles have a multiple of 1.5x to 2.0x. Marbles that are in very clear glass or marbles with bright colors have a multiple of 1.5 to 2.0x.

JOSEPH'S COAT SWIRLS
AND END-OF-DAYS

Joseph's Coat swirls are swirls that have a subsurface layer of glass that is composed of different colored strands, placed very closely together.

Generally, there are no or few clear spaces in between the strands. Some examples do have clear spaces. These can either be part of the design or just poor craftsmanship. There are usually some strands in the inner core that can be seen through the spaces. Generally, the more colors in the marble, the more valuable it is.

Joseph's Coat swirls have colors ranging from dark and earthy to bright English-style colors. They have a subsurface layer of bands and strands. Joseph Coat end of days have a subsurface layer of stretched bands.

The base glass of a Joseph's Coat can either be clear (#31, #32, #33, #34) or colored (#35, #36). Clear is much more common.

#31: Joseph's Coat end of day

#33: Joseph's Coat swirl

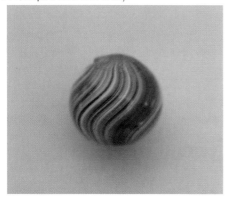

#32: Joseph's Coat swirl

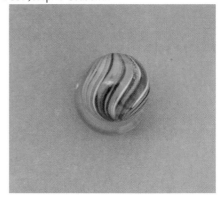

#34: Joseph's Coat end of day

#35: Joseph's Coat swirl in blue glass

#36: Joseph's Coat end of day in green glass

Joseph's Coat Swirls and End-of-Days

Size	Mint	Near Mint	Good	Collectible
1/2" or less	60.00	30.00	15.00	15.00
9/16" to 11/16"	75.00	40.00	15.00	5.00
3/4" to 1"	125.00	70.00	30.00	10.00
1" to 1-1/2"	275.00	100.00	45.00	25.00
1-5/8" to 1-7/8"	600.00	200.00	75.00	30.00
2" & over		Too Rare to Value		

These values are for marbles with clear base glass and earthy to pastel colors. Marbles with bright colors have a multiple of 1.25x to 2x. Marbles in colored glass have a multiple of 1.25x to 3x.

BANDED AND CORELESS SWIRLS

Banded and coreless swirls are swirls that have an outer or subsurface layer of bands or strands, but no inner core (#37, #38, #39, #40, #41, #42). These were intentionally made this way and are not errors. They are not as prized by collectors as other swirls, and therefore are not valued as highly

The outer layer on a banded swirl can be on the surface of the marble, or just under the surface.

Banded swirls are found with colored base glass (usually blue or green), about as often as they are found in clear. There is not much difference in value between the different colors.

Joseph's Coat swirls are a specialized variety of banded swirls. If the bands are very thin and packed closely together, then it is a Joseph's Coat swirl. Otherwise, it is a banded swirl.

#37: Coreless swirl (subsurface bands, clear glass)

#39: Banded swirl (surface bands, amber glass)

#38: Coreless swirl (subsurface bands, clear glass, viewed from top)

#40: Banded swirl (subsurface strands, clear glass)

#41: Banded swirl (surface strands, blue glass)

#42: Banded swirl (surface bands, blue glass, left-hand twist)

Banded Swirls

Size	Mint	Near Mint	Good	Collectible
1/2" or less	10.00	6.00	2.50	1.00
9/16" to 11/16"	15.00	10.00	4.00	2.00
3/4" to 1"	60.00	40.00	15.00	8.00
1" to 1-1/2"	110.00	75.00	50.00	20.00
1-5/8" to 1-7/8"	210.00	150.00	80.00	35.00
2" & over	375.00	200.00	100.00	60.00

Marbles with bright colors or well-designed outer layers have a multiple of 1.25x to 2x.

OTHER
CORE SWIRLS

There are several types of swirls that are specialized examples of banded or coreless swirls.

A gooseberry swirl is a transparent glass swirl with equidistantly spaced white subsurface strands. The base glass is usually honey amber (#43). There are also marbles with base glass that is green, clear or blue (#44). These are much rarer than the amber.

A caramel swirl (#45) is a marble with a dark transparent brown base glass and opaque white bands or swirls in it. Some examples have mica in them. These are rarer than those without mica.

Custard swirls (#46) and butterscotch swirls (#47) have wide translucent brown/pink strands on the surface. Custard swirls have a semi-opaque creamy yellow base. Butterscotch swirls have a semi-opaque creamy brown-yellow base.

Cornhusk swirls (#48) are a light transparent honey yellow glass with a single wide white band. They seem to be more common than the other swirls discussed above.

#43: Gooseberry swirl (amber)

#45: Caramel swirl

#44: Gooseberry swirl (clear)

#46: Custard swirl

#47: Butterscotch swirl

#48: Cornhusk swirl (green glass)

Miscellaneous Core Swirls

Size	Mint	Near Mint	Good	Collectible
1/2" or less	100.00	60.00	35.00	12.50
9/16" to 11/16"	70.00	50.00	25.00	10.00
3/4" to 7/8"	150.00	100.00	60.00	35.00
15/16" to 1-1/8"	275.00	200.00	100.00	50.00
1-1/4" to 1-7/8"	Too Rare to Value			
2" & over	Too Rare to Value			

These values are for amber gooseberry swirls, caramel swirls, custard swirls or butterscotch swirls. Gooseberries in a different color glass have a multiple of 3x to 8x. Cornhusk swirls have a multiple of 0.6x to 0.75x.

PEPPERMINT SWIRLS

A peppermint swirl is another specific type of banded swirl that has subsurface bands.

The marble has two wide opaque white bands, alternating with two thinner translucent blue bands. There are usually three (#49) or two (#50) transparent pink stripes on each white band.

Less common are marbles with a single transparent pink stripe on each white band. Some marbles exist that have two pink bands which are the same width as the two blue bands (#51, #52). These are called "beach ball" and are much rarer than the other types. There have also been a few marbles found with an odd number of pink bands (three or five). These are extremely rare (#53).

Marbles with mica in the blue bands are very rare (#54). There have also been some marbles found with a blue strand in one of the pink strands or with a green or pink strand in the blue band. These are also very rare, but do not seem to have any higher value.

#49: Peppermint swirl (four band)

#51: Peppermint swirl (two band)

#50: Peppermint swirl (six band)

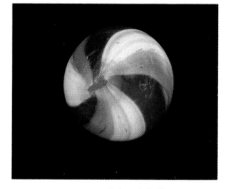

#52: Peppermint swirl (beach ball)

#53: Peppermint swirl (five band error)

#54: Peppermint swirl (four band with mica)

Peppermint Swirls

Size	Mint	Near Mint	Good	Collectible
1/2" or less	100.00	60.00	40.00	20.00
9/16" to 11/16"	75.00	45.00	25.00	15.00
3/4" to 1"	150.00	90.00	60.00	40.00
1" to 1-1/4"	500.00	300.00	200.00	100.00
1-3/8" to 1-7/8"	Too Rare to Value			
2" & over	Too Rare to Value			

These values are for peppermints with one, two or three pink stripes on each white band. "Beach ball" peppermints have a multiple of 1.25x to 2x. Marbles with mica in the blue bands have an additional multiple of 2.5x to 10x.

CLAMBROTHS

A clambroth is a swirl that has an opaque base with colored strands on the surface. The strands are generally equidistantly spaced.

The base color is usually opaque white. Some opalescent bases have been found. The most common colors for strands are pink, blue or green (#55). A clambroth that has strands of more than one color, usually alternating, is called "multicolored" (#56). These are rarer than the single-color marbles. Marbles with a base glass color that is not white, usually black (#57) or occasionally blue (#58) are also rare.

There are two different types of glass that were used for the base glass. One type is relatively hard, like other glass marbles, and does not chip easily. The other type is very soft and bruises quite easily. Some collectors believe that the hard type is German, while the soft type is early American. This does not appear to affect the value of the marble.

Missing strands or poor spacing of the strands results in a discount. Clambroths usually have eight to eighteen strands (depending on the marble size). There are some clambroths that have upwards of thirty or more strands. These are called "caged" clambroths (#59) and are rare. There are also clambroths that are "cased" in a layer of clear glass (#60) with a clear glass core.

#55: Clambroth (white base, green bands)

#57: Clambroth (black base, white bands)

#56: Clambroth (multicolored, white base, pink/blue/green bands)

#58: Clambroth (blue base, white bands)

#59: Clambroth (caged, white base, pink strands)

#60: Clambroth (cased, white base, red bands)

Clambroths

Size	Mint	Near Mint	Good	Collectible
1/2" or less	110.00	75.00	30.00	10.00
9/16" to 11/16"	140.00	90.00	40.00	20.00
3/4" to 7/8"	350.00	225.00	100.00	50.00
15/16" to 1-1/4"	500.00	300.00	175.00	100.00
1-3/8" to 2"	2,000.00	1,500.00	800.00	300.00
2-1/8" & over	Too Rare to Value			

These values are for marbles with white base and strands of a single color. Marbles with strands of two or more colors have a multiple of 1.25x to 2x. Marbles with a colored base have a multiple of 1.5x to 3.5x. "Caged" marbles have a multiple of 2x to 4x. "Cased" marbles have a multiple of 1.25x to 2x. Marbles with unusual or very bright colors have a multiple of 1.5x to 2x.

BANDED OPAQUES

A banded opaque has an opaque to transluscent base glass. The surface of the marble has colored strands, bands or stretched colored flecks on it.

A "swirl-type" banded opaque has colored strands and bands that are unbroken from pole to pole (#61). An "end-of-day-type" banded opaque has bands of stretched colored flecks on the surface (#62, #63). The stretched flecks generally are not continuous from pole to pole. One type does not seem to be any rarer than the other, but the "swirl-type" are valued slightly higher, probably because they tend to look better-designed.

Marbles with multi-color bands are rarer (#64), as are marbles with a color base glass, rather than the white base (#65). There are some marbles that have either a brightly colored base or brightly colored bands (#66). These are sometimes referred to as "electric" and are valued much higher than other banded opaques.

There is a rare type of banded opaque called a "Lightning Strike". This is a white base marble with several bands around the equator in several colors. The bands look like lightning bolts (#62). These have sold at auction for upwards of $5,000.

All else being equal, the greater the surface area that is covered by color, the more valuable the marble.

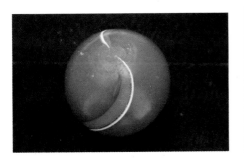

#61: Banded opaque (swirl type, top view)

#63: Banded opaque (end of day type

#62: Banded opaque (lightning strike)

#64: Banded opaque (end of day type)

#65: Banded opaque (end of day type)

#66: Electric banded opaque (end of day type)

Banded Opaques

Size	Mint	Near Mint	Good	Collectible
1/2" or less	100.00	60.00	30.00	15.00
9/16" to 11/16"	75.00	50.00	25.00	10.00
3/4" to 7/8"	125.00	75.00	50.00	25.00
15/16" to 1-1/8"	225.00	150.00	75.00	35.00
1-1/4" to 1-5/8"	350.00	225.00	125.00	75.00
1-3/4 & over		Too Rare to Value		

These values are for white based "end of day type" with a single color in the bands. "Swirl type" marbles have a multiple of about 1.25x to 1.5x. Marbles with a colored base have a multiple of 2x to 4x. Marbles with multi-color bands have a multiple of 1.5x to 3x. Marbles that are completely covered by color can have multiples of up to 5x. Marbles with very bright colors have a multiple of 1.5x to 3x higher. Lightning Strikes have a multiple of 6x to 15x.

INDIAN

An indian is a marble that has an opaque black base. On the surface are bands consisting of colored strands or stretched colored flecks.

A "swirl-type" indian has colored strands that run unbroken from pole to pole (#67, #68). Usually there is a colored band that consists of subsurface opaque white strands covered by a transparent color. An "end-of-day-type" indian has bands of stretched colored flecks that do not run continuously from pole to pole (#69, #70). "Swirl-type" indians are about as common as "end-of-day type" indians, but are valued more highly, probably because they seem to be better designed.

The surface usually has two bands on it. Multi-band examples are rarer and command a premium. Generally, the more surface area that is covered by color, the more valuable the marble (#71).

There are marbles with a translucent dark red or dark amethyst base glass. These are called "mag-lites" and carry a premium (#72). Blue, green or amber translucents are much rarer.

There are also marbles with transparent bases, generally green, blue or clear. A large (1-5/8") mint example sold in the fall of 2001 for $7,000.

#67: Indian (swirl type)

#69: Indian (end of day type)

#68: Indian (swirl type, top view)

#70: Indian (end of day type)

#71: Indian (end of day type)

Indians

Size	Mint	Near Mint	Good	Collectible
1/2" or less	60.00	30.00	15.00	5.00
9/16" to 11/16"	60.00	30.00	15.00	5.00
3/4" to 7/8"	200.00	75.00	40.00	15.00
15/16" to 1-1/8"	350.00	200.00	110.00	30.00
1-1/4" to 1-1/2"	1,250.00	750.00	300.00	100.00
1-5/8" & over		Too Rare to Value		

These values are for "end of day type" indians with two small bands of color. "Swirl type" indians have a multiple of about 1.1x. Indians with three or more bands have an additional multiple of 1.25x to 3x. Marbles that are completely covered with color can have a multiple up to 5x. "Mag-lites" have an additional multiple of 1.25x.

#72: Indian (end of day type, mag-lite, 360 degrees)

37

BANDED LUTZ

A banded lutz is a marble with a single-colored base glass and two sets of two bands alternating with two lutz bands. Lutz is finely ground copper flakes or goldstone. The lutz bands are usually edged by opaque white strands.

The term "lutz" derives from Nicholas Lutz, who was a glassworker at the Sandwich Glass factory. He used bands of goldstone in his glass. There is no evidence to suggest that marbles were made at Sandwich Glass, but the name has stuck.

The most common base glass is transparent clear (#73). Transparent color base glass (#74) is rarer. Semi-opaque base glass (usually colored) (#75) is very rare.

Opaque base glass (#76) is also rare. Marbles with opaque black bases are the most common of this type. Other colors (#77) are rarer.

A few rare examples have only two colored bands, rather than the usual four, or extra colored bands (#78). These are rare.

#73: Banded lutz (clear base)

#75: Banded lutz (semi-opaque green base)

#74: Banded lutz (green base)

#76: Banded lutz (opaque black base)

#77: Banded lutz (opaque white base)

#78: Banded lutz error

Banded Lutz

Size	Mint	Near Mint	Good	Collectible
1/2" or less	100.00	60.00	25.00	15.00
9/16" to 11/16"	100.00	70.00	40.00	20.00
3/4" to 1"	200.00	125.00	70.00	30.00
1-1/8" to 1-1/2"	350.00	250.00	150.00	60.00
1-5/8" to 2"	850.00	575.00	375.00	150.00
2-1/8" & over	1,500.00	750.00	450.00	275.00

These values are for marbles that have a clear base. Colored base marbles have a multiple of 1.5x to 3x. Semi-opaque base marbles have a multiple of 2x to 8x. Opaque black base has a multiple of 3x to 5x. Opaque "mag-lite" marbles have a multiple of 3x to 6x.

ONIONSKIN LUTZ

An onionskin lutz is a marble that has an end of day onionskin core with lutz bands and/or lutz sprinkled on the core.

The base color of the core is usually white, with blue, green or red streaks (#79, #80). Usually the streaks are not as pronounced as they are on an end of day that does not have lutz.

The lutz can vary from a light sprinkling on the core to very heavy lutz bands. Heavy lutz on the core (#81, #82) increases the value of the marble. In some instances, the lutz floats on a layer of clear glass above the core (#83). These are rare and are sometimes called "floaters."

Lobed and/or cloud (#84) examples are known to exist. These are very rare.

Marbles that have colored glass surrounding the core and lutz are also very rare. They are very difficult to value because of their rarity.

#79: Onionskin lutz (single color base)

#81: Onionskin lutz (heavy lutz)

#80: Onionskin lutz (multicolor base)

#82: Onionskin lutz (heavy lutz)

#83: Onionskin lutz (floater)

#84: Onionskin lutz (cloud)

Onionskin Lutz

Size	Mint	Near Mint	Good	Collectible
1/2" or less	175.00	110.00	50.00	20.00
9/16" to 11/16"	175.00	130.00	70.00	20.00
3/4" to 1"	400.00	300.00	150.00	70.00
1-1/8" to 1-1/2"	1,500.00	800.00	400.00	200.00
1-5/8" to 2"	3,250.00	2,000.00	900.00	450.00
2-1/8" & over		Too Rare to Value		

These values are for marbles with an average amount of lutz on the core. Marbles with heavy lutz have a multiple of 1.5x to 3x. "Floaters" have a multiple of 2x to 4x. Lobed or cloud marbles have a multiple of 3x to 6x. Marbles with colored base glass have an additional multiple of 3x to 6x.

41

RIBBON LUTZ

A ribbon lutz is a naked ribbon core swirl with lutz on both edges of the ribbon. There are single ribbon examples and double ribbon examples. No examples are known to exist that have an outer layer of strands or bands.

The basic type is transparent clear base with an opaque white single ribbon core (#85). The ribbon usually has transparent color glass over it (#86). There are some marbles with an opaque-color single ribbon (#87). These are somewhat rarer.

There are examples with a double ribbon, where each ribbon is a different color (#88).These are also somewhat rarer.

Some marbles are in transparent color glass (#89, #90). The ribbon is always opaque white. These are also somewhat rarer.

#85: Ribbon lutz (opaque white core)

#87: Ribbon lutz (transparent red on white core)

#86: Ribbon lutz (opaque orange core)

#88: Ribbon lutz (two-color core)

#89: Ribbon lutz (blue glass)

#90: Ribbon lutz (green glass)

Ribbon Lutz

Size	Mint	Near Mint	Good	Collectible
1/2" or less	350.00	150.00	60.00	40.00
9/16" to 11/16"	400.00	200.00	150.00	75.00
3/4" to 1"	600.00	350.00	250.00	100.00
1-1/8" to 1-1/2"	1,500.00	800.00	400.00	200.00
1-5/8" to 2"	3,250.00	2,000.00	900.00	450.00
2-1/8" & over		Too Rare to Value		

These values are for marbles with a clear base and a white ribbon with transparent color on it. Marbles with a colored ribbon have a multiple of 1.25x to 3x. Marbles with a different color on each side of the ribbon have a multiple of 1.252x to 3x. Marbles with colored base glass have a multiple of 1.25x to 4x.

INDIAN LUTZ

A swirl indian lutz (#91, #92) has an opaque black base with three lutz bands on the surface. The bands are edged with colored strands. An end of day indian lutz is a black core, which has stretched bands and strands of clolor on it, with a clear outer layer.

#91: Indian lutz (three bands)

#93: Indian lutz (end of day type)

#92: Indian lutz (three bands, top view)

Indian Lutz

Size	Mint	Near Mint	Good	Collectible
1/2" or less	900.00	350.00	225.00	100.00
9/16" to 11/16"	900.00	375.00	250.00	125.00
3/4" to 1"	3000.00	750.00	475.00	300.00

Over 1"   Too Rare to Value
(These values are for Swirl Indian Lutzes. End of day Indian Lutzes have a value about 0.5x)

MIST LUTZ

A mist lutz is a transparent clear base with a core of a transparent color. There is a layer of lutz just below the surface of the marble, floating between the core and the surface. Usually the core color is green (#94, #95). Several examples with red or black cores have been found and these are extremely rare (#96). There have also been some lutzes found that have a solid black core with lutz on the core itself. These are referred to as solid core lutzes and are valued the same as black mist lutzes.

#95: Mist lutz (green core)

#94: Mist lutz (green core)

#96: Mist lutz (black core)

Mist Lutz

Size	Mint	Near Mint	Good	Collectible
1/2" or less	300.00	200.00	150.00	50.00
9/16" to 11/16"	350.00	200.00	150.00	50.00
3/4" to 1"	700.00	375.00	225.00	150.00
Over 1"		Too Rare to Value		

These values are for Mists with a green core. Mists with a red or black core have a multiple of 1.5x to 3x. Marbles with heavy lutz have an additional multiple of 1.25x to 2x.

END OF DAY CLOUD

An End of Day Cloud has a transparent base glass, usually clear. The marble can have either a colored base core (#97) or no base core (#98). On the core are flecks of colored glass that were not stretched when the marble was drawn off the rod. This is different than an End of Day Onionskin, where the flecks of color did stretch.

Generally, the more colors, the more valuable the marble. Blue or red flecks on a white or yellow background is the most common. Yellow or green flecks, or a different colored background, are rarer.

Some marbles are left-hand twisted (#99). These are not as rare as Swirl marbles with a left-hand twist. Marbles with mica (#100) are not as rare as Swirls with mica. Some single-gather single-pontil marbles (#101) exist. These are rarer than cane-cut, although single-pontil clouds seem to be more common than single-pontil onionskins. Lobed marbles (#102) are also rare and have been found with three to six lobes.

#97: End of day cloud (white base core)

#99: End of day cloud (left-hand twist)

#98: End of day cloud (no base core)

#100: End of day cloud (lobed with mica)

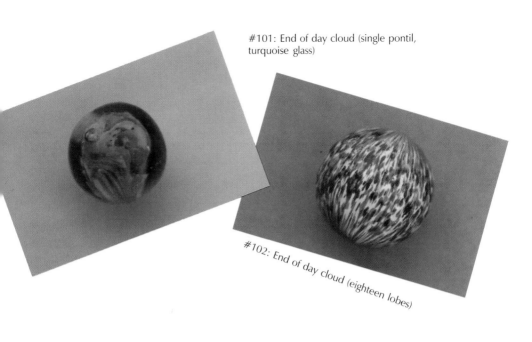

#101: End of day cloud (single pontil, turquoise glass)

#102: End of day cloud (eighteen lobes)

End of Day Cloud

Size	Mint	Near Mint	Good	Collectible
1/2" or less	40.00	20.00	10.00	5.00
9/16" to 11/16"	50.00	30.00	10.00	5.00
3/4" to 1"	100.00	75.00	50.00	20.00
1-1/8" to 1-1/2"	325.00	200.00	110.00	50.00
1-5/8" to 2"	500.00	250.00	125.00	60.00
2-1/8" & over	900.00	400.00	200.00	100.00

These values are for two-pontil, unpanelled clouds. Left-hand twist marbles have a multiple of 1.5x. Marbles with mica have a multiple of 1.5x to 3x. Lobed marbles have a multiple of 1.5x to 8x. Single pontil marbles have a multiple of 1.5x to 4x. Marbles with bright or unusual colors have a multiple of 1.5x. Marbles in colored glass have a multiple of 1.5x to 3x. Panelled marbles are discussed later.

END OF DAY ONIONSKIN

An End of Day Onionskin (#103, #104) has a transparent base glass, usually clear. The marble can have either a colored core or a transparent clear core. On the core are flecks of colored glass that were stretched when the marble was made.

Generally, the base color is white or yellow, and the flecks are red, blue or green. Other colors are rarer.

Some marbles are left-hand twisted (#105). This is not as rare as in Swirls. Marbles with mica (#106) are not as rare as in swirls. Single-gather, single pontil marbles (#107) are rarer than is seen with clouds. Lobed marbles (#108) have been found with three to eighteen lobes. These are also rare. Panelled marbles are relatively common and are discussed later.

#103: End of day onionskin (white base core)

#105: End of day onionskin

#104: End of day onionskin (yellow base core)

#106: End of day onionskin (with mica)

#107: End of day onionskin (single pontil, with mica)

#108: End of day onionskin (three lobes)

End of Day Onionskin

Size	Mint	Near Mint	Good	Collectible
1/2" or less	35.00	20.00	10.00	5.00
9/16" to 11/16"	35.00	20.00	10.00	5.00
3/4" to 1"	75.00	30.00	15.00	10.00
1-1/8" to 1-1/2"	175.00	100.00	40.00	20.00
1-5/8" to 2"	400.00	200.00	90.00	40.00
2-1/8" & over	900.00	400.00	150.00	80.00

These values are for unpanelled two-pontil onionskins. Left-hand twist marbles have a multiple of 1.25x to 2x. Marbles with mica have a multiple of 2x to 4x. Lobed marbles have a multiple of 1.5x to 8x. Marbles with bright or unusual colors have a multiple of 1.5x. Marbles in colored glass have a multiple of 1.5x to 3x. Panelled marbles are discussed later.

END OF DAY PANELLED CLOUD OR ONIONSKIN

An End of Day Panelled Cloud or Onionskin is a cloud or onionskin that has two or more distinct groups of colors.

The most common have four panels. Two of the panels are stretched red flecks on a white or yellow background, alternating with two panels of green or blue flecks on the background not used in the first panels. Panels of one colored flecks alternating with panels of different colored flecks, but all on the same color background are also fairly common. Other color combinations are rarer. About 90% of the panelled onionskins have four panels (#109). Other numbers of panels are rarer (#110).

Some marbles are left-hand twisted (#111). This is rare, although more common than in swirls. Some marbles have mica (#112), which is rare, and some are single-gather, single-pontil marbles (#113). There are some lobed marbles (#114). These are rare and usually the lobes mirror the panels.

Four panels adds a multiple of about 1.25x to 3x to the value of unpanelled clouds or onionskins, as shown on the previous two price tables. Multiple panels, other than four, are fairly rare and add a multiple of 2x to 6x to the value of the marbles shown in the previous two price tables.

#109: End of day panelled onionskin (four-panel)

#110: End of day panelled onionskin (six-panel)

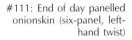

#111: End of day panelled onionskin (six-panel, left-hand twist)

#112: End of day panelled onionskin (four-panel, floating mica)

#113: End of day panelled onionskin (four-panel, single pontil)

#114: End of day panelled onionskin (four-panel, lobed, lobed with mica)

MIST

A mist is a transparent or translucent base with colored flecks of transparent or translucent glass stretched on the surface or just below it. The stretched colors can form bands or can completely cover the marble. However, the colors must be transparent or translucent, so that light shines through the marble.

Usually, the base glass is transparent clear (#115). However, other colored bases exist (#116). These are rarer than the clear base. The outer layer is usually colored, although examples of a colored base with clear mist have been found.

Occasionally, there is mica just below the surface of the marble (#117). This is relatively rare.

#115: Mist (surface bands, clear glass)

#116: Mist (surface bands, blue glass)

#117: Mist (subsurface bands, clear glass, with mica)

Mists

Size	Mint	Near Mint	Good	Collectible
1/2" or less	40.00	15.00	8.00	3.00
9/16" to 11/16"	50.00	25.00	8.00	3.00
3/4" to 7/8"	110.00	50.00	15.00	8.00
15/16" to 1-1/4"	200.00	75.00	40.00	15.00
1-3/8" to 1-5/8"	450.00	300.00	100.00	50.00
1-3/4" & over	Too Rare to Value			

The values are for transparent clear based mists. No surface color increases value by 1.5x to 2x. Colored bases increase the value by 1.25x to 2x. Mica in the marble increases the value by 2x to 4x.

SUBMARINE

A submarine is a difficult marble to categorize. They are cross between an end of day panelled onionskin, an indian, a mist and a banded swirl.

The base glass is always transparent. Either clear or colored (usually blue or green) (#118, #119, #120). There are two end of day panels of stretched colored flecks on the surface of the marble. These panels are on opposite sides and usually each covers about one-quarter of the marble. In the two resultant clear panels, there are stretched colored flecks below the surface of the marble. This creates a multi-layer effect.

Occasionally, there is mica just below the surface of the marble or in the panels or bands of mica, which is even rarer.

These marbles are rare and difficult to find.

#118: Submarine (green glass) #119: Submarine (green glass) #120: Submarine (blue glass)

Submarines

Size	Mint	Near Mint	Good	Collectible
1/2" or less		Too Rare to Value		
9/16" to 11/16"	300.00	125.00	75.00	25.00
3/4" to 7/8"	750.00	300.00	125.00	25.00
15/16" to 1-1/4"		Too rare to value.		
1-3/8" & over		Too Rare to Value		

Mica in the marble increases the value by 1.5x to 6x.

MICA

A mica marble is a transparent base glass with mica flakes in it.

The most common colors are clear, blue, aqua, brown and green (#121). Olive green and smoky gray are less common. Amethyst (#122) is rare. Yellow (#123) is rarer. Red micas (#124) are rarer than yellow.

Some micas have ghost cores (cores of tiny air bubbles) or thin dark filaments (#125). These are odd, but do not seem to add greatly to the value of the marble. Single-pontil, multi-layer, cased, single-gather or end-of-cane (#126) marbles are very rare and are valued higher.

A mica sold at the Philadelphia MarbleFest Auction on April 29, 1995. It was blue, 2-1/8" and Near Mint(+) (8.99). It sold for $3,490.

#121: Mica (blue)

#123: Mica (yellow)

#122: Mica (amethyst)

#124: Mica (red)

#125: Mica (filament core)

#126: Mica (cloud core, with mica)

Micas

Size	Mint	Near Mint	Good	Collectible
1/2" or less	12.50	8.00	5.00	1.00
9/16" to 11/16"	12.50	8.00	5.00	1.00
3/4" to 7/8"	40.00	30.00	15.00	8.00
15/16" to 1-1/4"	200.00	75.00	40.00	15.00
1-3/8" to 1-5/8"	500.00	200.00	100.00	50.00
1-3/4" & over		Too Rare to Value		

These values are for two-pontil, clear, blue, brown or green marbles. Aqua, olive-green or smoky-gray marbles have a multiple of 1.5x to 2.5x. Amethyst has a multiple of 3x to 5x. Yellow has a multiple of 7x. Red has a multiple of 10x to 20x. Ghost cores or core filaments add a multiple of 1.25x. Single-pontil marbles have a multiple of 4x to 6x.

SLAG, OPAQUE & CLEARIE

Slags

A slag (#127) is a marble made from a cane which is a mixture of black, brown, green or purple, and white glass. Rather than being a layered cane, like a Swirl, Slags are drawn off of a cane that is a mixture of two colors. Single pontil examples are covered in the transitional section.

#127: Handmade slag

Slags

Size	Mint	Near Mint	Good	Collectible
1/2" or less		Too Rare To Value		
9/16" to 11/16"	45.00	25.00	10.00	5.00
3/4" to 7/8"	70.00	40.00	25.00	10.00
15/16" to 1-1/4"	125.00	65.00	35.00	15.00
1-3/8" to 1-5/8"	225.00	120.00	60.00	25.00
1-3/4" & over	350.00	200.00	80.00	35.00

An opaque marble (#128, #129) is made from a rod of a single opaque color. White and black are the most common. Blue, pink and green are rarer. Other opaque or translucent colors are even rarer. Single pontil marbles, either single-gather or end-of-cane are very rare.

Opaques

There is also a type of opaque is made from a rod of two opaque or translucent colors (#130). The rod had one color (usually semi-opaque white) on one side and another color (usually semi-opaque green or blue) on the other. When the marble was twisted off the end, one side of the marble is one color and the other side is the other color. Because of the twisting motion, the marble looks like a machine-made corkscrew, but has two pontils, hence the name "handmade corkscrew." These are very rare.

#128: Handmade opaque

#129: Handmade opaque

#130: Handmade corkscrew

Opaques

Size	Mint	Near Mint	Good	Collectible
1/2" or less	10.00	5.00	2.00	1.00
9/16" to 11/16"	10.00	6.00	3.00	1.00
3/4" to 7/8"	35.00	15.00	7.50	3.00
15/16" to 1-1/4"	100.00	45.00	20.00	10.00
1-3/8" to 1-5/8"	150.00	65.00	30.00	15.00
1-3/4" & over	400.00	150.00	50.00	20.00

These values are for two-pontil black or white opaques. Blue, pink or green have a multiple of about 2x. Other colors have multiples up to 5x. Single-pontil marbles have an additional multiple of up to 5x. Handmade corkscrews have an additional multiple of 10x to 15x.

Clearies

A clearie marble (#131, #132) is made from a rod of a single transparent color. Clear is the most common, although light blue, light green and light amber examples are known. Single pontil examples, either single-gather or end-of-cane are rarer.

#131: Handmade clearie

#132: Handmade clearie

Clearies

Size	Mint	Near Mint	Good	Collectible
9/16" to 11/16"	20.00	8.00	3.00	1.00
3/4" to 7/8"	30.00	18.00	7.50	3.00
15/16" to 1-1/4"	65.00	30.00	20.00	10.00
1-3/8" to 1-5/8"	125.00	75.00	50.00	25.00
Over 1-3/4"		Too Rare to Value		

These values are for clear marbles. Other colors have a multiple of 2x to 3x. Single-pontil marbles have a multiple of 2.5x.

SULPHIDE

A sulphide marble has a transparent base with a ceramic-type figure inserted inside it. They are single-gather, single-pontil marbles.

The most common figure that is found in sulphide marbles is an animal (#133, #134, #135). Barnyard animals, household pets, squirrels and birds are most common. Wild animals including razorbacks, elephants and lions are a little less common.

Human figures (#136, #137) are more difficult to find. These can be either full length figures, or busts.

There is a series of sulphide marbles that contain the individual numerals 0 to 9 (#138).

There are also sulphide marbles with figures of inanimate objects in them (#139). These are usually coins, numerals on disks or pocketwatches. They are extremely rare.

Some sulphide figures are painted (#140). We have seen figures that are painted (simply or elaborately), as well as numerals and inanimate objects that are painted. The value of these is greatly affected by the degree of coverage, the brightness of the colors and the number of colors used.

Rarer still are sulphide figures in transparent colored glass (#141). A number of shades have been found, including blues, greens, yellows, amethysts, browns and pinks.

Also, extremely few sulphides have been found with more than one figure in them (#142). These are extremely rare.

The value of a sulphide is greatly affected by several factors, other than the type of figure in the marble. Because the figures were inserted into the glass by hand, the skill of the maker greatly affected the quality of the marble.

Figures that are off-center in the marble can be greatly discounted in value (by as much as 50%). A figure can either be too close to the right or left side of the marble, too high or low, or set too far forward or back.

The figure had to be heated to the same temperature as the glass on the end of the punty, in order for the marble to be made properly. If the temperature difference between the glass and the figure was too great, then the marble would shatter when it was being made. In some cases, the temperature difference was not so great that the marble would shatter, but rather the figure would crack when inserted. Cracked figures discount the value of the marble (by up to 50%). In other cases, pieces of the figure broke off when it was inserted into the glass. This also discounts the value.

In some cases, as the figure was being inserted into the marble, some air would be trapped in the marble as well. A thin layer of trapped air around the figure was necessary to achieve a silvery sheen that enhances the viewing of the figure. However, too much trapped air can cause so much reflection that the figure cannot be properly seen. Trapped air can discount the value of the marble by as much as 60%.

Finally, because sulphides are single-pontil marbles, there is always one pontil on the surface, that in some cases is ground down. If the pontil is on the bottom pole of the marble, then the figure can be viewed properly from all angles. However, depending on the skill of the maker, the pontil could end up anywhere on the marble in relation to the figure. In some instances, the pontil obscures viewing the figure. This can result in a discount on the value of the marble (up to 40%).

In 1993, a group of sulphides surfaced that have become the source of great controversy in the marble collecting community. These marbles have been dubbed "California Sulphides" because there was only one person who was selling them, and he was from California. Without getting into the whole history of the events surrounding the introduction of these marbles to the market, it is safe to say that the marble collecting community has been pretty much divided as to whether these marbles are as old as traditionally known sulphides, or are recent reproductions, or are older but not as old as antique sulphides. You must reach your own conclusions as to the age of these marbles.

California sulphides can be identified by several features. Many of them were in colored glass (usually very dark) or a light vaseline color. Many contained multiple figures (two or more). Many were figures that had never been seen before (seahorse, lady riding a horse side-saddle, etc.). None of the figures had a silvery sheen to them, and many had a light rust-red haze on them (#143). Very few of the marbles fluoresced under a black light (traditional sulphides usually fluoresce). Many had either a polished surface or an unpolished surface that had many tiny fissures in it when viewed by a 10x lens.

At this point, no one has been able to definitively prove that these marbles are new or old. You must draw your own conclusions.

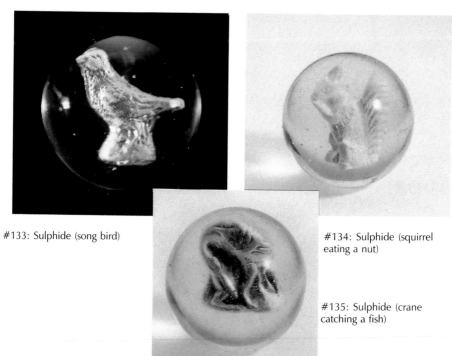

#133: Sulphide (song bird)

#134: Sulphide (squirrel eating a nut)

#135: Sulphide (crane catching a fish)

#136: Sulphide (man on a stump)

#140: Sulphide (painted bird on a stump)

#137: Sulphide (boy on a hobby horse, blowing a horn)

#141: Sulphide (seated lion in blue glass)

#138: Sulphide (#3)

#142: Sulphide (two fish)

#139: Sulphide (#6 on a disc)

#143: Sulphide ("California")

Sulphides

Size	Mint	Near Mint	Good	Collectible
23/32" or less		None Known to Exist		
3/4" to 7/8"	200.00	150.00	50.00	30.00
15/16" to 1-1/8"	150.00	100.00	50.00	30.00 .
1-1/4" to 2"	125.00	70.00	30.00	15.00
2" & over	200.00	100.00	50.00	30.00

These values are for common unpainted animals in transparent clear glass. Unusual animals are valued 1.25x to 3x higher. Human or mythical figures are valued 4x to 10x higher. Numerals are valued 3x to 6x higher. Inanimate objects are valued 5x to 10x higher. Multiple figures in the same marble are valued 3x to 10x higher. Painted figures or figures in colored glass are valued 10x to 20x higher.

#144: Paperweight marble

OTHER SINGLE-GATHER

Most varieties of cane-cut handmade marbles can also be found as single-pontil marbles. However, almost all of these are end-of-cane marbles, not single-gather marbles. A single-gather marble is a marble that was produced one at a time by adding successive layers of glass onto the end of a punty.

Several types of cane-cut marbles were also produced as single-gather marbles. These are End of Day Clouds, Micas and Opaques. However, the single-gather versions are much rarer than the cane-cut versions.

Aside from Sulphides, there is only one other type of marble that was produced solely as a single-gather marble. This is the Paperweight marble (#144). A Paperweight marble is a transparent glass base with small flecks or chips of colored glass forming a layer near the pontil of the marble. The marbles are rare. Almost all have a transparent clear base. I have only seen one with a transparent colored base, and that one was blue. The colored flecks are usually white, pink, yellow or green. Recently a group of these were found at a market in China. Collectors are divided as to whether these marbles are German, Bohemian or Chinese.

A rarer type of paperweight marble has a layer of millefiori canes where you would normally find the flecks of glass.

Paperweight

Size	Mint	Near Mint	Good	Collectible
1/2" or less		None Known to Exist		
9/16" to 11/16"	110.00	60.00	25.00	10.00
11/16" to 3/4"	175.00	85.00	60.00	25.00
13/16" to 15/16"	400.00	225.00	140.00	60.00
1" to 1-1/2"	600.00	400.00	200.00	100.00
Over 1-1/2"		None Known to Exist		

These values are for transparent clear base paperweight marbles. Colored base marbles have a multiple of 2x. Four-vane type have a multiple of 2x to 5x. Millefiori type have a multiple of 4x to 10x.

HANDMADE
NON-GLASS MARBLES

Serious collectors of handmade non-glass marbles are few and far between. Other than having a few examples of each type in their collections, most collectors do not pursue these marbles.

Clay and bennington marbles were produced by the millions, in both Germany and the United States, during the mid 1800s through the early 1900s. They were easy and cheap to produce, not requiring the technical knowledge or skill of glass marbles. The first marbles produced in the United States were clay marbles and the first marble-related U.S. patents are for devices that "mass produce" clay marbles.

While clays and benningtons are not in great demand, collectors are more interested in handpainted china marbles and agates. Some of the handpainted chinas are very colorful and beautiful. No marble collection is complete without a sampling. Handpainted chinas can also be quite rare. Scenic chinas rival most handmade glass marbles in terms of the price for rare examples.

No marble collection is complete without a sampling of hand-cut agates either. These marbles were the choice of marble shooters for many years, because of their ability to knock glass marbles out of the ring. Many hand-cut agates exhibit exquisite and complicated natural designs. A fine collection of different hand-cut agates could be created.

Another choice of some marble players was the steelie. These were preferred by players because their density could easily knock glass marbles out of a ring. However, they were banned from tournament play. Many steelies are merely ball bearings, but some are handmade hollow spheres that required a great deal of time to make. Every collection should have at least one handmade steelie.

In reality, handmade non-glass marbles do not get much attention by marble collectors. These marbles tend to get caught in the shuffle of the pursuit for the prettier and more colorful glass marbles. However, you should take your time and look at them while building your collection. They were an important part of the game of marbles for years and some of them are quite attractive.

CLAY

Clay marbles are the most common old marble that you will find. These marbles were the easiest to produce and millions still exist. Unfortunately, clay marbles do not have nearly the eye-appeal of any other marbles and therefore are the least collectible of any marble.

Clay marbles were made in both Germany and the United States. It has been reported that clay marbles were used as ballast in the keels of ships that sailed to America from Germany, and were then removed and sold in this country. On the American side, some of the earliest U.S. marble-related patents are for devices that fashion blobs of clay into round spheres, which were then fired to harden them.

Clay marbles are usually found in their natural tan color (#145), but they may also be dyed. The dyed marbles are usually found in red, blue, brown, green or yellow (#146). Foil clays are small (usually less than 1/2" diameter) clays with a metallic coating on them. These were produced in Germany after the turn of the century and are usually found in Mosaic games. Unfortunately, none of these clays has much value because they are so common.

#145: Clay (natural)

#146: Clay (dyed)

Clay

Size	Mint	Near Mint	Good	Collectible
1/2" or less	0.01	N/V	N/V	N/V
9/16" to 11/16"	0.01	N/V	N/V	N/V
3/4" to 1"	0.05	0.01	N/V	N/V
1-1/8" to 1-1/2"	0.15	0.10	0.02	N/V
1-5/8" to 2"	1.50	1.00	0.25	0.10
Over 2"	5.00	2.50	1.00	0.50

These values are for natural tan color clays. Dyed clays have a multiple of 2x to 3x.

CROCKERY

Crockery marbles are a type of clay marble that is made from two or three different colors of clay. Some are merely opaque white or off-white marbles that were fired at a higher temperature than clays, making them somewhat denser. There are also some lined crockery that are opaque white with thin blue and/or green swirls mixed in (#147). These are harder to find.

The lined crockery marbles were made by rolling together the different colors of clay. You can achieve the same effect today with a little experimentation with Sculpty® clay. Crockery marbles were all fired to harden them. There are glazed and unglazed varieties of crockery marbles. Some have very intricate designs in the swirl patterns.

#147: Crockery (lined)

Crockery

Size	Mint	Near Mint	Good	Collectible
1/2" or less	10.00	5.00	1.00	0.50
9/16" to 11/16"	15.00	5.00	3.00	1.00
3/4" to 1"	75.00	30.00	10.00	3.00
1-1/8" to 1-1/2"	150.00	90.00	25.00	5.00
1-5/8" to 2"		None Known to Exist		
Over 2"		None Known to Exist		

These values are for glazed lined crockery marbles. Opaque white or off-white marbles without colored swirls are valued with a multiple of 2x to 3x over the Clay price table. Unglazed marbles have a multiple of about 0.5x. Unusual patterns or large amounts of blue and/or green have multiples of 3x to 5x.

BENNINGTON

Bennington marbles are a type of glazed clay marble. They are not very dense. The marbles are fired clay with a salt glaze on them. Benningtons are readily identifiable by both their coloring and the little "eyes" that they have on them. These are spots where the marbles were touching each other while they were being fired, resulting in those spots being uncolored and unglazed.

The term "bennington" is actually a misnomer. There is no evidence that they were ever made in Bennington, Vermont, or that they have any lineage to the Bennington pottery that they resemble and from which they get their name. It appears that all Bennington marbles were imported from Germany. Boxes have been found that contain them and that are labeled "Agates - Imitation / Made in Germany."

Benningtons are usually colored brown or blue (#148). Marbles that have both brown and blue on them, as well as a little green, are referred to as "fancy benningtons" (#149). These are rarer than the single color variety. Pink, gray, green or black benningtons have also been found.

#148: Bennington

#149: Fancy bennington

Bennington

Size	Mint	Near Mint	Good	Collectible
1/2" or less	0.25	0.02	N/V	N/V
9/16" to 11/16"	0.30	0.05	N/V	N/V
3/4" to 1"	1.00	3.00	1.00	N/V
1-1/8" to 1-1/2"	10.00	7.50	3.00	0.50
1-5/8" to 1-7/8"	25.00	17.50	8.00	1.00
Over 2"		Too Rare To Value		

These values are for blue or brown benningtons. Green benningtons have a multiple of 2x to 4x. Fancy benningtons have a multiple of 5x to 10x. Pink, gray, green or black benningtons have a multiple of 10x to 25x.

STONEWARE

Stoneware marbles are a dense, fired clay marble with salt glaze on them (#150).

These marbles are made in the same manner as salt-glazed stoneware crocks and jugs and may very well have been made by the same makers. The marbles have similar blue patterns on them. Usually the patterns are spongeware-type or splatterware-type, or else they tend to be bands encircling the equator.

These marbles are fairly rare, although not as valuable as their rarity would suggest, probably due to their lack of eye appeal.

#150: Stoneware

Stoneware

Size	Mint	Near Mint	Good	Collectible
1/2" or less	None Known To Exist			
9/16" to 11/16"	15.00	8.00	3.00	1.00
3/4" to 1"	50.00	17.50	10.00	2.00
1-1/8" to 1-1/2"	100.00	75.00	50.00	15.00
1-5/8" to 2"	300.00	200.00	100.00	50.00
Over 2"	None Known to Exist			

CHINA

China marbles are marbles that are made with a very dense white clay and then fired at a very high temperature. This produces a much heavier marble, for the size, than a clay or crockery marble. Most chinas are painted. Some of the decorations can be quite intricate. Many of the chinas that you will find are glazed as well. Jeff Carskadden has written an excellent book on china marbles (see bibliography) and you should refer to it for a more detailed description of the different types.

In order of rarity, painted chinas have the following patterns: Lines (#151) on one axis, helix on pole or poles, intersecting lines, crows feet (#152), bullseyes (#153), simple flowers, donut hole flowers, roses (#154), intricate roses (#155), scenic designs (#156). Some handpainted chinas have been found with gold-colored bullseyes. These are rare.

A 1-1/8" intricate rose china, similar to #155, was sold by A Chip Off The Old Block in its Internet Cyberauction in 1998 for $6,925.

#151: China (lined)

#153: China (bullseye)

#152: China (crow feet)

#154: China (rose)

#155: China (intricate rose)

#156: China (scenic)

China

Size	Mint	Near Mint	Good	Collectible
1/2" or less	15.00	5.00	2.00	0.50
9/16" to 11/16"	15.00	8.00	3.00	1.00
3/4" to 1"	45.00	15.00	5.00	2.00
1-1/8" to 1-1/2"	125.00	50.00	15.00	4.00
1-5/8" to 2"	175.00	85.00	40.00	22.00
Over 2"	250.00	125.00	65.00	30.00

These values are for glazed lined marbles. Marbles with a helix on one or both poles have a multiple of 1.5x. Crows feet have a multiple of 2x. Bullseyes have a multiple of 2.0x. Simple flowers have a multiple of 50x. Donut hole flowers have a multiple of 8x. Roses have a multiple of 10x to 20x. Intricate roses have a multiple of 50x to 150x. Scenic designs have a multiple of 100x to 300x. Unglazed marbles have a multiple of 0.50x.

CARPET BALL

Carpet balls are glazed, crockery spheres that are used in a game similar to bocce. Most carpet balls are believed to have been made in England or Scotland, where the game was very popular.

Many carpet balls are in the 3" to 3-1/2" range. They have varying designs painted on them. Some of the designs (from most common to least common) are: Lined, intersecting lines-single color (#157), intersecting lines-multiple colors, crown and thistle (#158), flower, mochaware. Mochaware tend to be slightly smaller. There is a small sized (about 2-1/4") opaque white ball that is called the jack. This was the target ball. Sometimes, the name of a store is printed on them. There were also lady-sized balls (about 2-1/2"). These are less common.

Recently, many reproductions have begun to appear. These can be identified by several features: They have a thick clear glaze; many have small circular hit marks that just crack the glaze; and if they have small chips then the interior is a dark white or tan color (original carpet balls have chalky white interiors).

#157: Carpet ball (intersecting lines)

#158: Carpet ball (crown and thistle)

Carpet Balls

Size	Mint	Near Mint	Good	Collectible
2-1/4" (Jack)	60.00	20.00	10.00	5.00
2-1/2" (Child or lady)	100.00	75.00	40.00	20.00
3" to 3-1/2"	100.00	75.00	40.00	20.00

These values are for lined carpet balls. Intersecting lines of a single color have a multiple of 1.25x. Intersecting lines with multiple colors have a multiple of 1.5x. Crown and thistle have a multiple of 1.6x. Flowers have a multiple of 2x. Mochaware has a multiple of 5x. Jack balls that are imprinted with a store name have a multiple of 1.6x.

AGATE

Agate is a colored variety of quartz that was hand-ground into marbles. They were a favorite of many marble players, especially as shooters. This is because agates are denser than other marbles. This made it easier to knock an opponent's marble out of the ring.

Hand-cut agates are generally found in banded (#159) and carnelian (#160) varieties. The banded varieties have distinct concentric rings on the sphere. They command a value that is about double the carnelian examples. Carnelians are a more uniform brownish-red color. Many agate marbles have subsurface moons because of their extensive use as shooters.

There are many machine-ground agates available (#161). These are modern. Hand-cut agates have tiny facets on the surface. You can see the light dance on the surface if you look closely at the surface while turning the marble. There are also dyed agates available (#162). Some of these are older, handcuts and some are modern. A chemical process and pressure is used to accentuate the brightness of the natural colors. Usually they are found in green, blue and black and occasionally in yellow.

#159: Agate (hand-cut, banded)

#161: Agate (machine ground)

#160: Agate (hand-cut, carnelian)

#162: Agate (dyed)

Agates

Size	Mint	Near Mint	Good	Collectible
1/2" or less	7.50	3.00	1.00	0.25
9/16" to 11/16"	7.50	3.00	1.00	0.25
3/4" to 1"	12.50	5.00	2.00	1.00
1-1/8" to 1-1/2"	20.00	10.00	5.00	2.00
1-5/8" to 2"	40.00	20.00	10.00	5.00
Over 2"	60.00	35.00	15.00	7.50

The above are values for hand-cut, carnelian agates. Hand-cut banded agates have a multiple of 2x to 5x. Machine-ground agates have a multiple of .25x to .33x. Machine ground dyed agates have a multiple of 3x to 5x. Hand-cut dyed agates have a multiple of 10x to 20x.

OTHER MINERAL

There are many mineral spheres available. Most of these are not true marbles, but merely minerals in the spherical shape. Almost all are modern.

Some marble collectors add these to their collections because they display well. However, most of these were never intended to be used to play the game of marbles, although some were produced to be used in solitaire-type games.

The only mineral, except agate, that is known to have been used to produce marbles in any significant quantity is limestone. This is a white or off-white, fairly dense mineral. They were produced extensively in Germany and used there, as well as the United States, during the late 1700s to the early 1900s. They have a value similar to clays (see above).

A number of other mineral spheres are available. Among the more readily available are tigereye (#163), onyx (#164), goldstone (#165), malachite (#166), snowflake obsidian (#167), rhodenite (#168). The value of each is determined by their relative rarity as a mineral. Representative values are:

#163: Tigereye sphere

#164: Onyx sphere

#165: Goldstone sphere

#167: Snowflake obsidian sphere

#166: Malachite sphere

#168: Rhodenite sphere

Other Mineral

Size	Mint	Near Mint	Good	Collectible
1/2" or less	7.50	3.00	1.00	0.25
9/16" to 11/16"	10.00	8.00	3.00	1.00
3/4" to 1"	20.00	10.00	4.00	1.50
1-1/8" to 1-1/2"	35.00	12.00	5.00	2.00
1-5/8" to 2"	50.00	18.00	7.50	2.50
Over 2"	75.00	25.00	12.50	5.00

OTHER MATERIALS

Handmade marbles were also produced from wood, paper and steel.

Wooden marbles can be found in either their natural color or dyed. They were probably not used in marble playing because they are not very dense, and therefore not very effective for shooting or targets. They have little value to collectors.

Marble collectors come across a number of steel marbles in their hunting. Most of these are solid ball bearings. These have little value to marble collectors.

However, there are some handmade steelies available. These are hollow steel spheres that were made by hand. They can be identified by their lightness and by the "X" on one end where the open end was folded (#169). Occasionally, they may have rust, but clean examples are collectible. Marbles that are 5/8" to 11/16" and Mint have a value of about $10.00. Steelies that are 3/4" to 1" and Mint have a value of about $25. Larger hollow steelies are very rare.

There is also a type of marble that seems to be constructed from paper mache (#170). These are very rare. They are very light and were probably meant for use in a board game and not in marble shooting games.

The marbles usually are a red, orange and black swirl pattern. I have seen very few of these. Damaged examples have revealed that the marbles are constructed of layers of paper with some kind of binding material, paste, or glue.

Sizes range from 5/8" to 7/8". Representative values are 5/8" ($150), 3/4" ($250), 7/8" ($450).

#169: Hollow steelie

#170: Paper mache marble

MACHINE-MADE MARBLES

Until about 15 years ago, machine-made marbles were not considered collectible by many marble collectors. Most collectors ended up with machine-made marbles as part of collections that they were buying because they wanted the handmade marbles in them. They would generally throw the machine-made marbles in a box and forget about them. Very little attempt was made to identify or classify the many different types of machine-made marbles, either by appearance or by manufacturer. There were some notable exceptions to this, especially in the area of Akro Agate Company or Peltier Glass Company marbles. But, for the most part, machine-made marbles were not given much serious attention by the majority of collectors.

For several reasons, all of that began to change during the mid-1980s. An influx of new collectors into the hobby created a demand for handmade marbles that had not previously existed. This increased the prices of handmade marbles. As those prices began to move up at a rapid rate, collectors found that they could acquire many beautiful and colorful machine-made marbles for the price of a single handmade marble.

Another reason that machine-made marbles began to receive more attention was related to their historical significance. Virtually all handmade marbles were made in Germany and then imported into the United States (as well as other countries). Machine-made marbles were almost exclusively an American product for the first half of the 20th century. The rise of the American marble manufacturers mirrors in many ways the rise of the United States as an economic force. Many examples of original packaging still exist, making it easy to identify the different types and manufacturers of machine-made marbles. An interest arose in documenting and preserving this period of American toy manufacturing.

The final reason for the increased interest in machine-made marbles was nostalgia. By the mid-1980s, the kids who had played with mibs, aggies and commies in the playground had grown up. As occurred with many other collectibles over the past two decades, collectors began buying back the objects of their youth that had been lost to numerous location changes or indifference.

So, by the late 1980s, the time and environment were ripe for an explosion of interest in machine-made marbles. The catalyst for this explosion was the publication in 1990 of the book *Collectable Machine Made Marbles* by Larry Castle and Marlowe Peterson. Previously (since 1976), the Marble Collectors Society of America had published identification sheets and prices for machine-made marbles, but the Castle and Peterson book was the first attempt to classify all types of machine-made marbles by manufacturer.

Since the publication of the Castle and Peterson book, the number of people collecting machine-made marbles has grown by leaps and bounds. This increased interest and demand has seen the publication of several additional books on machine-made marbles or their manufacturers (see the bibliography for a complete list).

In the following section on machine-made marbles, we will discuss the identification and valuation of marbles by company. .

TRANSITIONAL

Transitional marbles are among the earliest American-made marbles. The term "transitional" applies to most slag-type marbles that have one pontil. These marbles were probably made by one of several processes. Some were made by gathering a glob of molten glass from a pot onto the end of a punty and then either rounding a single marble off the end or allowing the glass to drip off the end of the punty into a machine as another worker cut the stream to create individual globs of glass. It is also likely that some later transitionals were actually made completely by machine. In this case, the stream of glass came out of a furnace, through a shearing mechanism, and then went into a crude set of rollers that rounded the marbles, but did not rotate them around all axes. As a result, the cut-off mark from the shearing mechanism remained.

The marbles are collectively called "transitional" because many were made partly by hand and partly by machine. Thus, they represent a bridge between handmade marbles and machine-made marbles.

Several American companies produced transitional marbles. Most of the companies were short lived. Among the more well known companies are Navarre Glass Company and M.F. Christensen & Son Company. Some collectors believe that "Leighton" transitionals were produced mainly in Germany, and some crease pontil transitionals were produced in Japan or the far East, and that some regular pontil transitionals were produced in China.

Transitional marbles are usually identified by the type of pontil. Some are also identified by the manufacturer, but this can be difficult, at best.

All transitionals are slag-type marbles. They are a colored transparent glass with translucent or opaque white mixed in. There are a few marbles that are a transparent clear glass with colors swirled in. These are commonly called "Leighton" marbles (#171) and are rare. The swirled colors are usually white, yellow, pink, lavender and/or oxblood.

There are eight basic types of pontil: Regular (#172, #173), Ground (#174, #175), Melted (#176, #177), Pinpoint (#178), Fold (#179, #180), Pinch (#181) and Crease (#182).

Regular pontil transitionals (#172, #173) have a pontil on one end that looks just like the pontil on a handmade marble. This type is fairly rare. It is likely that many of these were not even made using any type of machine. Rather, they were individually hand-gathered on a punty and then rounded in a device and sheared off.

#171: Transitional ("Leighton")

#172: Transitional (regular pontil)

#173: Transitional (regular pontil)

Regular Pontil Transitional

Size	Mint	Near Mint	Good	Collectible
Less than 3/4"	50.00	25.00	7.50	3.00
3/4" to 1"	75.00	30.00	10.00	3.00
1-1/8" to 1-1/2"	125.00	60.00	20.00	10.00
1-3/8" to 2"	275.00	125.00	40.00	15.00
Over 2"	400.00	200.00	50.00	20.00

"Chinese" transitionals have a multiple of 0.1x

Ground pontil transitionals (#174, #175) have a pontil on one end that has been ground and faceted. Many of these are Regular pontil transitionals that the manufacturer took the time to grind the pontil off of. They command about the same prices as Regular pontil transitionals, but they are not quite as rare. Some varieties of Ground pontil transitionals have oxblood and/or bright yellow or white swirled in. These are referred to as "Leighton" marbles (#171), because it is popularly believed that an early marble-maker named James Leighton developed the colors used in these. The "Leighton" transitionals are very rare. Recently, some re-worked glass transitionals with oxblood have appeared. Please see the reproduction section of the guide for information on those marbles.

#174: Transitional (ground pontil)

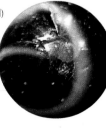

#175: Transitional (ground pontil)

Ground Pontil Transitionals

Size	Mint	Near Mint	Good	Collectible
Less than 3/4"	50.00	25.00	10.00	5.00
3/4" to 1"	90.00	40.00	15.00	8.00
1-1/8" to 1-1/2"	175.00	75.00	40.00	15.00
1-5/8" to 2"	350.00	140.00	75.00	20.00
Over 2"	500.00	225.00	100.00	50.00

"Leighton" marbles have a premium of 2.6x to 6x.

Melted pontil transitionals (#176, #177) are more common than either Regular pontils or Ground pontils. These are marbles that have a pontil on one end that has been partially melted into the marble. The pontil was either melted manually over a flame or else was melted into the marble surface while the marble was being formed in the early marble-making machine. Most Melted pontil transitionals exhibit either a "9 and swirl pattern" or else a looping pattern where the white runs in a band or bands from the pole, over the top of the marble, and back to the pole. It is generally believed that the "9" pattern was made by the M.F. Christensen & Son Company and that the looping pattern was made by the Navarre Glass Company. However, since the glass for these marbles was hand-gathered, it may very well be that they were simply made by different gatherers in the same factory. The "9" pattern marbles (marbles where the white glass on the top pole forms a "9") seem to be a little more common than the loop pattern marbles.

#176: Transitional
(melted pontil)

#177: Transitional
(melted pontil)

Melted Pontil Transitionals

Size	Mint	Near Mint	Good	Collectible
Less than 3/4"	30.00	10.00	5.00	2.00
3/4" to 1"	80.00	30.00	10.00	3.00
1-1/8" to 1-1/2"	150.00	50.00	15.00	4.00
1-5/8" to 2"	225.00	65.00	30.00	12.50
Over 2"	350.00	100.00	45.00	20.00

Pinpoint pontil marbles (#178) are very rare. Occasionally, Melted pontil transitionals or Pinch pontil transitionals are confused with Pinpoint pontil transitionals. The pontil on these marbles is characterized by a very tiny pontil that looks almost like the head of a pin. The pontil on these marbles was formed because the glass was a little too cool when it was sheared off the punty and dripped into the machine. As a result, the cut-off spot did not completely melt into the marble because the marble cooled too quickly as it was forming. These pontils are very rare. Occasionally, they are found on marbles that are made from two opaque colors of glass, rather than a transparent and opaque color.

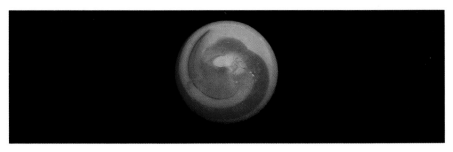

#178: Transitional (pinpoint pontil)

Pinpoint Pontil Transitionals

Size	Mint	Near Mint	Good	Collectible
Less than 3/4"	60.00	25.00	10.00	5.00
3/4" to 1"	125.00	65.00	30.00	10.00
Over 1"		None Known to Exist		

Fold pontil transitionals (#179, #180) are also rarer than Melted pontils. The pontil is characterized by a tiny finger of glass that is folded over at the cut-off point and partially melted into the marble surface. This pontil is formed by a similar process to the Pinpoint pontil. The glass was a little too cool when it was sheared off into the machine. As a result, the cut-off spot did not completely melt into the marble because the marble cooled too quickly as it was forming.

#179: Transitional (fold pontil)

#180: Transitional (fold pontil)

Fold Pontil Transitionals

Size	Mint	Near Mint	Good	Collectible
Less than 3/4"	40.00	15.00	5.00	2.00
3/4" to 1"	110.00	50.00	20.00	5.00
Over 1"		Too Rare To Value		

     Pinch pontil transitionals exhibit a short straight raised line on the bottom pole. Usually, the top pole has a 9" type configuration. The cut-off line on a pinch pontil is much straighter and usually much shorter than that seen on the crease pontils discussed below. Crease pontils usually are about a 1/5 to 1/4 the circumference of the marble. Pinch pontils are usually less than 1/10 the circumference of the marble. It is likely that pinch pontil transitionals are American marbles, and that the pontil is the remnants of a mechanized shearing process, rather than a hand-cut process. Many have bright colors and there has been speculation that some are early Christensen Agate Company.

     Crease pontil transitionals (#181, #182) are fairly common. It is not known whether these were made by an American company or in Japan or the Far East. These marbles are characterized by a spidery crease line that runs along the entire bottom of the marble. Again, the mark was formed because the glass was too cool when it was sheared off as it was dripping into the marble-making machinery. These marbles tend to be transparent blue, aqua, green or brown, with a bright opaque white swirls in and on them.

#181: Transitional (crease pontil)

#182: Transitional (pinch pontil)

Pinch or Crease Pontil Transitionals

Size	Mint	Near Mint	Good	Collectible
Less than 3/4"	15.00	5.00	2.00	1.00
3/4" to 1"	50.00	20.00	10.00	4.00
Over 1"		None Known to Exist		

These are values for transparent color base with opaque white swirl. Opaque white base with translucent swirl have a multiple of 1.25x to 1.5x.

     Almost all marbles sent to us by collectors, that they have identified as various transitional pontils, are actually cold roll seams on common swirls, clearies and opaques. Transitional marbles are always an older slag-type marble.. "Transitional type" markings on common swirls and other types from the 1930s and later are just artifacts of the glass stream being too cold when the marble was formed, and are not transitional marks.

M.F. CHRISTENSEN
& SON COMPANY

The M.F. Christensen & Son Company operated in Akron, Ohio, from 1904 until 1917. Martin Christensen patented the first marble-making machine. Many M.F. Christensen marbles are transitionals, because the glass was gathered by a punty and dripped by hand over the rotating machine. The machinery rounded the marble. M.F. Christensen machines did not have automatic feed systems. The molten glass had to be hand-fed off a punty into the machinery. Later M.F. Christensen marbles do not have pontils. This is probably due to refinements in the glass temperature and timing, rather than improvements in the machinery. It is very doubtful that the company ever developed automatic feed or shearing mechanisms.

M.F. Christensen marbles are strictly single-stream marbles. They are either single-color opaque or two-color slag. This is because the glass for a particular batch was all mixed in one furnace pot and not the separate streams used by later manufacturers. Interestingly, there do not appear to be any M.F. Christensen & Son Company marbles that exhibit a distinctive set of three colors. The company seems to have confined itself to marbles of only one or two color.

The M.F. Christensen & Son Company produced some opaque marbles (Photo #183). These appear to have been made in limited quantity. Some of these are transitionals. A close examination of M.F. Christensen opaque marbles reveals a faint "9" on the top pole. Generally, you can find them in green ("Imperial Jade"), light blue ("Persion Turquoise") and yellow. There were some lavender opaques produced, but they are very rare. We have been approached by many collectors who thought that they had M.F. Christensen opaques, when the marbles were really common game marbles. In fact, the purple marbles are very, very rare and it is very difficult to assign a value to them.

#183. M.F. Christensen Company Persion Turquoise

M.F. Christensen & Son Company Opaques

Size	Mint	Near Mint	Good	Collectible
1/2" or less		Too Rare to Value		
9/16" to 11/16"	150.00	110.00	40.00	10.00
23/32" to 25/32"	300.00	140.00	65.00	15.00
7/8" to 1"		Too Rare to Value		
Over 1"		Too Rare to Value		

The most common M.F. Christensen & Son Company marbles are slags (#184). These marbles have a swirling pattern of transparent colored base with opaque white swirls. Most M.F. Christensen & Son Company slags have a "9" pattern on the top pole and the "cut-off line" on the bottom. These patterns are caused by the twisting motion used in hand gathering the glass out of the furnace and keeping the glass on the end of the punty as a stream of it was allowed to drip into the machine. The marbles are found in blue, green, brown, purple, orange, aqua, yellow and clear. M.F. Christensen slags are found in a wide array of shades of each of the colors mentioned. The brown and purple are the most common, perhaps they were the easiest or cheapest to make. The blue and green are next most common, and are fairly easy to find. Clear and aqua are more difficult. Occasionally, the aqua marbles will have a little bit of oxblood in them. Yellow is the second hardest to find and "true" orange and light lavender are the most difficult color to find. Generally, the better defined the "9", the more valuable the marble. Also, the brighter and clearer the base transparent color, the more highly valued is the marble. Some of these marbles are truly beautiful. The value for slags varies greatly depending on the craftsmanship exhibited in the "9" and the rarity of the hue of the color. There is a wide variation in hues, even within one color, of M.F. Christensen slags. This variation is much more pronounced than you see in other manufacturers. It is not known if this was intentional, or the result of the company's inability to accurately replicate color formulas.

#184: M.F. Christensen & Son Company "9" slags

M.F. Christensen & Son Company Slags

Size	Mint	Near Mint	Good	Collectible
1/2" or less	5.00	1.00	0.35	0.10
9/16" to 11/16"	7.50	2.00	0.45	0.15
23/32" to 25/32"	30.00	10.00	3.50	0.25
7/8" to 1"	75.00	15.00	5.00	1.25
1-1/8" to 1-3/8"	175.00	60.00	12.50	3.00
Over 1-1/2"	400.00	125.00	45.00	20.00

These values are for amber or purple marbles. Blue or green have a multiple of 1.5x, clear and aqua are 4x, yellow are 7x and orange and lavender are 10x.

M.F. Christensen & Son Company made a type of slag that is different than the others. This slag is referred to today as the oxblood slag (#185), although it has been reported that the company named them "moss agate." In reality, the marble looks more like bloodstone than moss agate. The marble is a very dark transparent green base glass with a swirl of oxblood in and on it. Usually, the oxblood forms a "9" and has a tail on the other end. These marbles are often overlooked as just dark opaque game marbles because the base glass is so dark and the oxblood does not really stand out. However, closer examination reveals the oxblood. These marbles are fairly rare. Some collectors call these "green bricks."

#185: M.F. Christensen & Son Company oxblood slag

M.F. Christensen & Son Company Oxblood Slags

Size	Mint	Near Mint	Good	Collectible
1/2" or less		None Known to Exist		
9/16" to 11/16"	150.00	60.00	20.00	5.00
23/32" to 25/32"	300.00	110.00	40.00	15.00
Over 1-1/4"		Too Rare to Value		

The most popular M.F. Christensen & Son Company marble is the Brick (#186, #187) . It was called the "American Cornelian" by the company. The marble is a combination of oxblood-red and opaque white, opaque black or translucent green or a combination of any or all. The common name for the Brick derives from the fact that the marble looks like a piece of brick when it is scuffed up. Because they were handgathered, each marble is unique in its coloring and pattern. The oxblood-red with black are a little rarer than the oxblood-red with white. Oxblood-red with dark transparent green are very hard to find. The most highly sought after examples have well-defined "9"s and tails. Many examples do not have "9"s at all and some collectors believe that these are either very late examples or perhaps marbles that were made later by the Akro Agate Company. There are also some very early examples that are transitionals and have a pontil. These are extremely rare and the values are multiples higher than the values listed below.

#187. M.F. Christensen Company Brick

#186: M.F. Christensen & Son Company brick

M.F. Christensen & Son Company Bricks

Size	Mint	Near Mint	Good	Collectible
1/2" or less		Too Rare to Value		
9/16" to 11/16"	60.00	25.00	10.00	5.00
23/32" to 25/32"	85.00	50.00	15.00	7.00
7/8" to 1"	250.00	120.00	50.00	25.00
1" to 1-1/8"	325.00	175.00	90.00	40.00
Over 1-1/8"		Too Rare to Value		

These values are for oxblood-red with white. Oxblood-red with black have a multiple of 1.10x. Bricks with dark green have a multiple of 2x to 4x.

CHRISTENSEN AGATE COMPANY

The Christensen Agate Company was founded in 1925 in Payne, Ohio. In 1927, the company moved to Cambridge, Ohio, and was located in a small building near the Cambridge Glass Company. The company had no connection with Martin Christensen or the M.F. Christensen & Son Company. However, the original incorporators may have felt that the use of the Christensen name was a good marketing move.

Christensen Agate produced a variety of marble styles. These marbles were distributed by the company itself, through the J.E. Albright Company of Ravenna, Ohio, and through the Gropper Company of New York City.

The Christensen Agate Company produced only single-stream marbles in all varieties: single-color, slag and swirl. It does not appear that any Christensen Agate marbles are variegated stream. Many Christensen Agate marbles are made with very brightly colored glass. These are referred to as "electric" colors. The glass colors are unique to Christensen Agate marbles and command much higher prices than the normal colors. Christensen Agate marbles can exhibit either two seams (on opposite sides of the marble), a single seam (e.g., a diaper fold) or no seam. There is very little known about the techniques the company actually used to produce marbles, so it is unclear if different machinery or techniques produced each type of marble.

It does appear that some Christensen Agate marbles are hand-gathered. For at least a short period of time early in the company's history, marbles were hand-gathered prior to the implementation of an automatic shearing system. We have found slags and swirls that exhibit hand-gathered "9"s and tails. Many American Agates exhibit these features.

Christensen Agate Company produced a single-stream marble that they called the "World's Best Moon." This is a translucent white opalescent marble (#189). The marble is similar in appearance to the Akro Agate Moonie. It can be identified as a Christensen Agate marble by two features. First, the Christensen Agate version tends to be brighter than the Akro Agate version and have a slightly bluish tinge to it. Second, the Christensen Agate version tends to have tiny air bubbles inside it, which the Akro version does not. The Christensen Agate Moon is valued comparable to the common slags valued velow. There is a Christensen Agate Moon that is light blue (#190). These are very rare and have a multiple of 3x to 5x.

Christensen Agate produced slags (#191, #192) in a variety of colors. These are transparent color base marbles with opaque white swirls in them. The pattern must be a transparent color base with opaque white. If the marble is two opaque colors, then it is considered a swirl. Also, the opaque white should be randomly swirled through the marble and the surface. If the white is banded or striped on the surface, with only a little inside, it is probably a striped transparent. Generally, the colors of Christensen Agate slags are much brighter than those produced by other manufacturers. Some of the slags have an "electric" color base (#193), usually orange or yellow, which is rarer than the non-"electric" colors. The rarest color is peach, which was not made by any other company (#194).

#189: Christensen Agate Company Moon

#192: Christensen Agate Company red slag

#190: Christensen Agate Company Blue Moon

#193: Christensen Agate Company electric slag

#191: Christensen Agate Company aqua slag

#194: Christensen Agate Company peach slag

Christensen Agate Company Slags

Size	Mint	Near Mint	Good	Collectible
1/2" or less	25.00	10.00	2.00	1.00
9/16" to 11/16"	25.00	10.00	5.00	2.00
23/32" to 25/32"	60.00	25.00	15.00	7.50
7/8" to 1"	110.00	50.00	40.00	20.00
Over 1"		None Known To Exist		

These values are for common-color slags (green, purple, amber). Aqua or red have a multiple of 1.10x to 1.5x. Orange has a multiple of 1.25x to 2.0x. Yellow has a multiple of 1.5x to 2.25x. Peach has a multiple of 3x to 5x. "Electric" colors have an additional multiple of 2x to 5x.

The most common Christensen Agate Company marbles are Swirls. Christensen Agate produced swirls in a wide variety of different patterns and color combinations. The marbles were made by mixing two or more glass colors in a single furnace. Because each color was a different density, they did not melt together, but rather created strata. Since the molten glass was the consistency of molasses, the individual stratum remained as the glass was turned into marbles. There are an almost endless variety of colors and patterns in Christensen Agate swirls. Most swirls are in the 9/16" to 3/4" range. Peewees and marbles over 3/4" are very rare.

White based swirls are the most common, but there are also many examples of swirls with no white in them. The marbles can be two-color (#195) or multiple colors (#196). There do not seem to be any swirls with more than five colors in them. Generally, each color is opaque, although there are some marbles that have at least one transparent color (#197). The colors can also be dull, or very bright. Bright colors are referred to as "electric."

Occasionally, the swirl patterns form a row, or two opposing rows, that look like the flames that were painted on the sides of hot rods during the 1950s. Marbles with these patterns are called Flames (#198, #199) by collectors today and are rare.

Another rare type of swirl is the transparent swirl (#200). These are a transparent base with another color swirled in. The second color can be opaque, translucent or transparent. That color is usually electric. Clear is the most common base color, with some green, yellow or blue examples known. The most common swirl colors are yellow and orange. Lavender has also been seen. These marbles are fairly rare.

#196. Christensen Agate Company Swirl

#195: Christensen Agate Company tri-color electric swirl

#197: Christensen Agate Company transparent electric swirl

#199. Christensen Agate Company Flame Swirl

#198: Christensen Agate Company two-color flame

#200: Christensen Agate Company transparent swirl

Christensen Agate Company Swirls

Size	Mint	Near Mint	Good	Collectible
1/2" or less	15.00	5.00	2.00	1.00
9/16" to 11/16"	20.00	8.00	4.00	2.00
23/32" to 25/32"	45.00	20.00	10.00	5.00
7/8" to 1"	200.00	60.00	30.00	10.00
Over 1"		None Known To Exist		

These values are for swirls of two common opaque colors, where one color is white and where the patterns are average. Three-color swirls have a multiple of 2x to 3x. Four-color swirls have a multiple of 3x to 5x. Marbles that do not have white as one of the colors have an additional multiple of 1.5x to 2x. Transparent swirls or swirls with "electric" colors have an additional multiple of 3x to 8x. Flames have an additional multiple of 3x to 15x, depending on the number of flame points and the intricacy of the pattern.

There are some swirls that have specialized names. Bloodies (#201), which is the name used by the company, are an opaque white base with transparent red and translucent brown swirls. These are rarer than we had originally thought and have a multiple of 3x to 5x the previous price table. American Agates (#202), again the name used by the company, are an opaque white to opalescent white base with a swirl that ranges from translucent electric red to transparent electric orange. These have a multiple of 1.5x to 3x the previous price table. Diaper-fold (#203), a name applied by collectors today, refers to a swirl that is a single seam pattern. When viewed from the

#202. Christensen Agate Company American Agate

#201. Christensen Agate Company Bloodie

side, the swirl pattern looks like a diaper on a baby. These have an additional multiple of 1.25x to 1.5x to a comparably colored swirl. Turkey (#204), another name applied by collectors today, is a swirl pattern that looks like the head of a turkey. These have an additional multiple of 1.25x to 1.5x a comparably colored swirl.

Christensen Agate Company also produced a marble similar to the swirls. These were an opaque base with a series of color bands on the surface of one side of the marble, and little or no color on the other side or inside. Often, the band colors are "electric" and the base can be either opaque or transparent. These are referred to as Striped Opaques (#205) and Striped Transparents (#206).

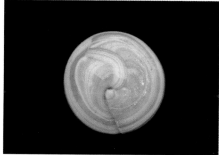

#203: Christensen Agate Company diaper-fold swirl

#205: Christensen Agate Company striped opaque

#204: Christensen Agate Company turkey swirl

#206: Christensen Agate Company striped transparent

90

Christensen Agate Company
Striped Opaques & Transparents

Size	Mint	Near Mint	Good	Collectible
1/2" or less	15.00	6.00	2.00	1.00
9/16" to 11/16"	40.00	15.00	8.00	2.00
23/32" to 25/32"	100.00	40.00	20.00	7.50
7/8" to 1"		Too Rare to Value		
Over 1"		None Known To Exist		

These values are for average-color marbles. "Electric" colors or intricate patterns have a multiple of 1.5x to 3x.

The "World's Best Guineas" (#208) are a transparent based marble with colored flecks of glass melted and stretched on the surface. Occasionally, you will see these flecks inside the marble, particularly in seamed examples (Guinea-Cobra). We have been told that the name Guinea originated because the marble colors looked like the heads of the Guinea Cocks that ran around the factory yard. The most common base color is clear, followed by cobalt and then amber. Some green based Guineas have surfaced, but these are very rare. I have also been told of a couple of red based Guineas that exist, but have never seen them. The value of a Guinea is also affected by the number of colors on the surface and the intricacy of the pattern. The largest Guinea known is 15/16". One was sold for $2,125 in October 1993 at an auction by Block's Box. Cobras (sometimes called Cyclones) (#209) look like Guineas with all the stretched flecks of colored glass inside the marble. They have only been found in clear base and transparent blue. There is a marble referred to as a Guinea Cobra hybrid (#207). This marble is a Guinea with color inside the marble. Unfortunately, there are several different types of fake Guineas that have produced in the past couple of years. See the chapter on Reproductions for more details.

#207: Christensen Agate Company Cobra

#208: Christensen Agate Company Guinea

#209: Christensen Agate Company Cobra

Christensen Agate Company
Guineas & Cobras

Size	Mint	Near Mint	Good	Collectible
1/2" or less	600.00	225.00	100.00	50.00
9/16" to 11/16"	325.00	225.00	150.00	50.00
23/32" to 25/32"	600.00	325.00	200.00	75.00
7/8" to 1"	3,000.00	2,000.00	750.00	425.00
Over 1"		None Known to Exist		

These values are for clear Guineas. Cobalt base has a multiple of 1.1x, amber base has a multiple of 1.25x. Cobras and Guinea-Cobras have a multiple of 1.5x to 3x .

AKRO AGATE COMPANY

The Akro Agate Company was formed in 1910 in Akron, Ohio. It was moved to Clarksburg, West Virginia, in 1914, where it remained until its bankruptcy in 1951. The company originally repackaged marbles bought from the M.F. Christensen and Son Company. By the time the company had moved to Clarksburg, it was operating its own marble making machinery and producing marbles.

Throughout most of the history of the company, Akro Agate was the largest manufacturer of marbles in the United States. The company introduced a number of improvements and design changes to its machinery, which yielded several different types of marbles that could not be replicated by competitors. Many Akro Agate marbles are very collectible today.

The company produced both single-stream and variegated stream marbles in all types, except ribboned and veneered.

As with many of the other manufacturers of the time, Akro Agate produced a staggering number of single-color marbles. They produced both clearies, which are transparent clear or transparent colored glass marbles, and opaques, which are opaque colored glass marbles. These marbles have little value today for several reasons. First, they were produced in such mass quantity that they are abundantly available. Second, since they were the easiest marble to produce, every marble company produced them. It is virtually impossible to distinguish between each company's marbles of this type. Finally, because the marbles are only one color, they do not have much eye appeal. Akro referred to their early opaque marbles as "Opals".

The exception to this are a series of opaques that were produced with opalescent glass. Opaque marbles of white opalescent glass were called Flint Moonies by the company and are referred to today as Moonies (#210). Opaque marbles of colored opalescent glass are referred to collectively as Flinties. Brown (#211) is the most common, followed by yellow, green, red and blue. These marbles are actually semi-opaque and have a distinctive orangish glow when held to a light. Later examples have tiny open ends at either pole, called "fisheyes". The Moonies are relatively easy to find. The Flinties are more difficult. It appears that Flinties were not produced in as great quantities as Moonies and these marbles are often mistaken for game marbles by collectors. Flinties can be found in many No. 150 and No. 200 tins. They were also marketed under the name "Fire Opal."

#210: Akro Agate Company Moonie

#211: Akro Agate Company Flintie (brown)

Akro Agate Company Moonies and Flinties

Size	Mint	Near Mint	Good	Collectible
1/2" or less	10.00	4.00	1.00	0.25
9/16" to 11/16"	10.00	4.00	1.50	0.50
23/32" to 25/32"	25.00	15.00	5.00	2.00
7/8" to 1"	65.00	35.00	10.00	6.00
Over 1"		None Known To Exist		

These values are for Moonies and brown Flinties. Yellow and green Flinties have a multiple of 1.25x. Red Flinties have a multiple of 1.5x. Blue Flinties have a multiple of 2x.

The other single-stream marble that Akro Agate produced was the slag (#212, #213, #214, #215). Akro Agate produced a large quantity of slags. It would be a fair statement that there are more Akro Agate slags available than those of the three other slag manufacturers (M.F. Christensen, Christensen Agate and Peltier) combined. The most common color is amber, followed by purple, blue, green, red, aqua, clear, yellow and orange.

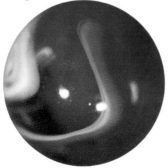

#212: Akro Agate Company blue slag

#213: Akro Agate Company green slag

 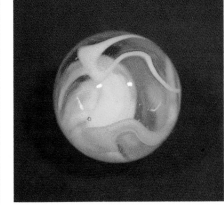

#214: Akro Agate Company red slag   #215. Akro Agate Company yellow slag

Akro Agate Company Slags

Size	Mint	Near Mint	Good	Collectible
1/2" or less	10.00	4.00	1.00	0.25
9/16" to 11/16"	1.25	0.30	0.05	0.01
23/32" to 25/32"	5.00	2.00	0.50	0.10
7/8" to 15/16"	25.00	10.00	3.50	1.50
31/32" to 1-3/16"	60.00	25.00	10.00	3.00
Over 1-1/4"		Too Rare To Value		

These values are for amber, purple, blue or green slags. Red have a multiple of 3x, aqua and clear have a multiple of 4x, yellow has a multiple of 6x and orange has a multiple of 10x.

Akro also made a single-stream opaque-type of slag called the Cornelian. This marble is a combination of opaque red and white glass, and is very similar to a Brick. The color is not as oxblood-red as a Brick though. Cornelians are rare. In Mint condition, they are valued at $50 for 5/8" examples, up to $100 or more for 13/16" examples. I have never seen any larger than 7/8". There is evidence from recent digs at the Akro site that the company produced bricks. These are a darker red than M. F. Christensen bricks and are valued the same as M. F. Christensen bricks.

Akro Agate produced several different types of variegated-stream swirls. Some of these swirls that are collectible today were produced in the same colors as the corkscrew "Ades" (discussed below). However, the most collectible are the oxbloods. Oxblood actually refers to a specific color that is found on the marble. This is a deep rust red with black filaments in it. The color is very similar to dried blood, hence the name. It is often confused with red colors of other manufacturers. However, those colors are almost always translucent to transparent and do not have black filaments. Oxblood must be opaque and it must have black filaments in it.

Oxbloods are found in corkscrew, swirl or patch varieties. They are usually referred to by the name of the underlying marble that they are found on: Chocolate oxblood (opaque brown or dark tan base with oxblood) (#219), milky oxblood (translucent white base with oxblood) (#216), silver oxblood (translucent silver base with opaque white swirls and oxblood), limeade oxblood (limeade corkscrew with oxblood) (#217), egg yolk oxblood (milky white base with a bright yellow swirl and oxblood) (#218), carnelian oxblood (Carnelian Agate with oxblood) (#220), blue oxblood (milky white base with a translucent blue swirl and oxblood) (#221), orange oxblood (milky white base with translucent orange swirls and oxblood), lemonade oxblood (milky white base with yellow swirl and oxblood) (#222), oxblood corkscrew (opaque white base with an oxblood corkscrew, sometimes on a dark blue spiral, which is called a blue-blood) (#223), swirl oxblood (white base with oxblood swirls) (#224), patch oxblood (white base with a stripe of oxblood on one side) (#225). The swirl and patch oxbloods are generally believed to be more recent than the others. Also, some hybrid examples (#226) which are combinations of two of the above have been found, but they are extremely rare. Generally, the oxblood floats on the surface of the marble. It is less common to find some of the oxblood inside the marble. Examples smaller than 9/16" and larger than 7/8" are extremely rare, (except for patch oxbloods).

#216. Akro Agate Company chocolate oxblood

#219: Akro Agate Company chocolate oxblood

#217. Akro Agate Company limeade oxblood

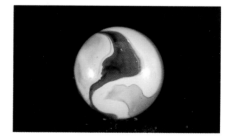

#220: Akro Agate Company carnelian oxblood

#218. Akro Agate Company egg yolk oxblood

95

#221: Akro Agate Company blue oxblood

#224: Akro Agate Company swirl oxblood

#225. Akro Agate Company patch oxblood

#222. Akro Agate Company lemonade oxblood

#226: Akro Agate Company hybrid oxblood (egg yolk and blue)

#223: Akro Agate Company oxblood corkscrew ("blueblood")

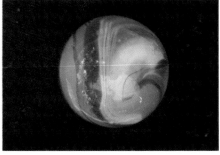

#227: Akro Agate Company hybird oxblood (egg yolk and blue)

Akro Agate Company Oxbloods

Size	Mint	Near Mint	Good	Collectible
1/2" or less		Too Rare To Value		
9/16" to 11/16"	6.00	3.00	1.00	0.25
23/32" to 25/32"	15.00	9.00	3.00	1.00
7/8" to 15/16"	30.00	18.00	8.00	5.00
31/32" to 1"		Too Rare To Value		
Over 1-1/16"		None Known To Exist		

These values are for patch oxbloods. Swirl oxbloods have a multiple of 3x, milky oxbloods, silver oxbloods and oxblood corkscrews have a multiple of 6x (if the oxblood is on top of a blue corkscrew, a "blueblood", then the value is about 7x), lemonade, blue and carnelian oxbloods have a multiple of 7x to 12x, egg yolk oxbloods have a multiple of 9x to 15x, limeade and orange oxbloods have a multiple of 10x to 30x, clear oxbloods, chocolate oxbloods and hybrid oxbloods have a multiple of 12x to 45x.

The most common and easily recognizable Akro Agate marble is the corkscrew. This is a variegated-stream marble whose design is unique to Akro Agate. Two or more streams of colored glass were allowed to enter through the marble-making machine's shearing mechanism at the same time. Because the different colors were layered as they came out of the furnace and because the colors were of different densities, they created separate strata in the glass stream as it entered the shearing mechanism. Just before the shearing mechanism in the Akro machinery there was a small cup with a hole in the bottom. The glass stream entered the cup from the top and passed through the hole in the bottom into the shearing mechanism. If the cup was spinning, then a corkscrew was created. If the cup was not spinning, then a patch was created. The number of different colored spirals in the corkscrew, or the number of different color patches was determined by the number of nozzles that had glass flowing through them when the glass stream was created.

Corkscrews are identifiable as being two or more spirals of color that rotate around the marble from one pole to the other, but do not intersect. Different color combinations and designs were marketed by Akro Agate under a variety of names: Prize Name (two opaque colors) (#228, #229), Special (three or more opaque colors) (#230), Ace (one opaque color and translucent milky white) (#231), Spiral (transparent clear base with colored spiral) (#232), Onyx (transparent color base with opaque white spiral) (#233). In addition, other names have been applied by children and collectors over the years: Snake (a Spiral or Onyx where the opaque or colored glass is on the surface and just below it) (#234, #235), Ribbon (a Spiral or Onyx where the opaque or colored glass goes almost to the center of the marble) (#236), "Ades" (types of Aces with fluorescent base glass) (#237, #238, #239), and Popeye (a specific type of Special commonly found in Popeye marble boxes) (#240, #241, #242, #243, #244, #245).

Two-colored white-based Prize Names are the most common corkscrew type. This is followed by two-colored color-based Prize Names, Onyx, Spirals, three-color Specials, Aces, four-color Specials and five-color Specials. Although I have heard of six color corkscrews, I have never actually seen an example where the sixth color was not actually a blend of two of the other colors. If a true six-color Special exists, then it is extremely rare. Any corkscrew over 1" is rare. The first price table is for two-colored white-based Prize Names (with multiples listed for other types), the second price table is for Popeyes and the third price table is for "Ades." The color and design combinations of corkscrews is almost limitless. You could easily amass a collection of several hundred corkscrews, of which no two would be the exact same color combination or pattern. Odd color combinations or patterns are usually worth several times the values listed in the tables below.

#228: Akro Agate Company two-color corkscrew (Prize Name, white base)

#231: Akro Agate Company translucent corkscrew (Ace)

#229: Akro Agate Company two-color corkscrew (Prize Name, color base)

#232: Akro Agate Company transparent corkscrew (Spiral)

#230: Akro Agate Company three-color corkscrew (Special)

#233: Akro Agate Company transparent corkscrew (Onyx)

#234: Akro Agate Company snake corkscrew (Spiral)

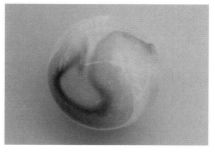

#237: Akro Agate Company lemonade (swirl type)

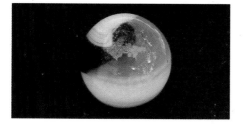

#235: Akro Agate Company snake corkscrew (Onyx)

#238: Akro Agate Company limeade (corkscrew type)

#236: Akro Agate Company ribbon corkscrew (spiral)

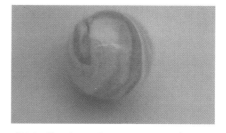

#239: Akro Agate Company orangeade (corkscrew type)

Akro Agate Company Corkscrews

Size	Mint	Near Mint	Good	Collectible
1/2" or less	5.00	1.50	0.25	0.05
9/16" to 11/16"	1.50	0.50	0.10	0.05
23/32" to 25/32"	8.00	2.00	0.50	0.25
7/8" to 15/16"	17.50	6.00	2.50	1.50
31/32" to 1"	40.00	15.00	7.50	4.00
Over 1-1/16"		Too Rare To Value		

These values are for two-colored white-based Prize Names. Two-colored color-based Prize Names have a multiple of 2x to 4x, Onyx and Spirals have a multiple of 3x to 10x, three-colored Specials and Aces have a multiple of 5x to 15x, four-colored Specials have a multiple of 6x to 40x, five-colored Specials have a multiple of 10x to 75x.

Popeye corkscrews are a three-, four-, or five-color Special that contain a unique color spiral. This unique color is transparent clear with filaments of opaque white. The filaments can almost completely fill the transparent clear or they can be sparse. The most common colors, in addition to the clear/white, are red and yellow (#240) or green and yellow. These are followed (in order of increasing rarity) by red and green (#241), dark blue and yellow (#242), light purple and yellow, dark purple and yellow (#243), powder blue and yellow, red and blue (#244), red and orange, orange and green, blue and green, black and yellow, or various hybrid colors (#245). Hybrid Popeyes are marbles that have three or four colors along with the clear/white. It is popularly believed that these marbles occurred when the colors were changed in one of the machine hoppers. However, some of these examples are too perfectly formed to be an accident. They may have been intentionally made by using five nozzles, instead of four, to create the glass stream. There are some Popeye corkscrews that have a fourth color that is really just a blending of the two colored glass streams. These really are not hybrids. True hybrids are rare and are highly prized by collectors.

Some Popeyes were produced when the spinning cup in the machine was not rotating. As a result, these marbles came out as patches. They are the same color combinations as Popeyes, but are actually two or three distinct patches of color on a clear/white base. These are called Patch Popeyes (#248) and are very rare. They have been easily confused with a type of Vitro Agate patch, and have fallen out of favor with collectors at this time.

There are also several types of corkscrews that have a similar clear/white color combination as Popeyes, but only one other colored spiral (usually translucent red or orange) These are usually referred to as Ringers (#246) or Imperials (#247) and are not really Popeyes. They would be valued about the same as two-color Aces.

#240: Akro Agate Company Popeye corkscrew (red/yellow)

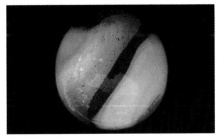

#242: Akro Agate Company Popeye corkscrew (blue/yellow)

#241: Akro Agate Company Popeye corkscrew (red/green)

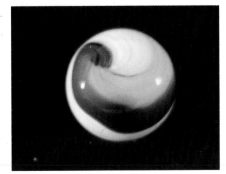

#243: Akro Agate Company Popeye corkscrew (purple/yellow)

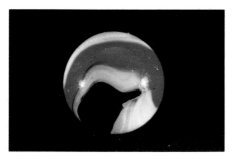

#244: Akro Agate Company Popeye corkscrew (red/blue)

#246. Akro Agate Company Ringer

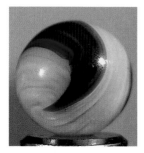

#245. Akro Agate Company hybrid Popeye corkscrew

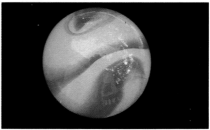

#247: Akro Agate Company Imperial

Akro Agate Company Popeye Corkscrews

Size	Mint	Near Mint	Good	Collectible
1/2" or less		Too Rare To Value		
9/16" to 11/16"	22.50	12.00	3.50	0.50
23/32" to 25/32"	45.00	25.00	10.00	2.50
7/8" to 15/16"	350.00	100.00	40.00	20.00
31/32" to 1"	500.00	200.00	100.00	50.00
Over 1-1/16"		Too Rare To Value		

These values are for red and yellow or green and yellow examples. Red and green have a multiple of 1.25x, dark blue and yellow have a multiple of 1.75x, light purple and yellow have a multiple of 2.5x, dark purple and yellow have a multiple of 3x to 5x, powder blue and yellow, red and blue or red and orange have a multiple of 5x to 10x, blue and green have a multiple of 7x to 12x, black and yellow have a multiple of 18x, and hybrid colors have a multiple of 5x to 25x.

The "Ades" are also a specialized type of corkscrew. These are a corkscrew that consists of a fluorescent milky off-white glass with filaments of opaque white and a spiral of a translucent color. If the color is yellow then it is called a lemonade (#237), green is called a limeade (#238), orange is called an orangeade (#239), red is called cherry-ade, and brown is called a Carnelian (#249). The Carnelian is the only one that is actually the name used by Akro Agate. Some of these marbles are really swirls, and not distinctive corkscrews. This does not affect the value.

#248: Akro Agate
Company Popeye
patch (red/green)

#249: Akro Agate
Company Carnelian Agate

Akro Agate Company "Ade" Corkscrews

Size	Mint	Near Mint	Good	Collectible
1/2" or less		Too Rare To Value		
9/16" to 11/16"	12.00	4.00	1.50	0.50
23/32" to 25/32"	18.00	8.00	3.50	1.25
7/8" to 15/16"	40.00	17.50	7.50	2.50
31/32" to 1"	65.00	30.00	12.50	7.50
Over 1-1/16"		None Known To Exist		

These values are for lemonade corkscrews. Carnelian Agates have a multiple of 2x, limeade corkscrews have a multiple of 2x to 4x, and orangeade and cherryade corkscrews have a multiple of 4x to 6x.

Another type of machine-made marble that has several variations which are uniquely Akro Agate are patches. A patch is a corkscrew that was not twisted. It is a variegated stream of glass consisting of two or more colors.

There are several types of patches that Akro Agate marketed under various names, including Hero (Photo #250), Unique, Moss Agate (#251), Royal (#252) and Helmet (#253). The Hero and Unique are the oldest type of Akro Agate patch. These appear to have been produced for a short period of time during the mid-1920s. Both marbles are an opaque white base with a wispy brown patch brushed on about one-third of the marble. The Unique has a small space in the middle of the patch through which the white base shows. The Hero does not have this space. Both of these are readily identifiable because they have a crimp mark at either pole which indicates that they were produced before the Freese Improvement (see glossary). This would date them to the early to mid 1920s. Moss Agates are a two-color patch. One color is a fluorescent translucent milky brownish/white base. The other color is a translucent colored patch (generally brown, yellow, red, blue or green) which covers one-quarter to almost one-half the marble. An Akro Royal is a two-color patch. The base color is opaque. The patch is either opaque or transparent and usually covers about one-quarter of the marble. An Akro Helmet is a three-color patch. The base glass is a transparent color. The patch is an opaque color covering about half the marble. Usually it is white. There is usually a colored stripe brushed on the middle of the patch. When viewed from the proper angle, the marble looks like a striped football helmet sitting on top of a head, hence the name. It does not appear that Akro actually marketed this marble under the name Helmet Patch. There is discussion amongst collectors that Helmet Patches may actually have been made by Vitro Agate Company.

102

#250: Akro Agate Company Hero

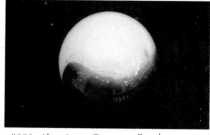

#252: Akro Agate Company Royal

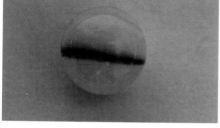

#251: Akro Agate Company Moss Agate

#253. Akro Agate Company helmet patch

Akro Agate Company Patches

Size	Mint	Near Mint	Good	Collectible
1/2" or less		Too Rare To Value		
9/16" to 11/16"	1.00	0.25	0.05	0.01
23/32" to 25/32"	2.00	0.60	0.15	0.05
7/8" to 15/16"	4.00	1.50	0.50	0.20
31/32" to 1"	7.50	4.00	1.25	0.50
Over 1-1/16"		None Known To Exist		

These values are for Akro Specials. Moss Agates and helmet patches have a multiple of about 4x to 8x. Heros and Uniques have a multiple of 25x to 50x.

Another type of marble that is unique to Akro Agate is the Sparkler (#254). This is a clear base marble with filaments and strands of various colors running inside the marble from pole to pole. It appears to be made using the same technique as some cat's-eyes, in that various colors of glass are injected into a clear stream as it flows through the furnace. However, Sparklers pre-date all other cat's-eyes by at least 15 to 20 years. Sparklers were produced in the mid to late 1920s and do not appear to have been produced much past 1930. They have generally only been found in the 5/8" to 3/4" size. Sparklers are often confused with clear Master Marble Sunbursts (#255). They can be differentiated by several features. Sparklers tend to have brighter colors than Sunbursts. Also, Sparklers usually have five different colors in them, whereas Sunbursts have at most three different colors. There is also another marble that is very similar to

Sparklers and is usually referred to as a "foreign sparkler" (#256). These can be 9/16" to 1" and are a transparent clear base with translucent strands of color running through the center or brighter colors running as a ribbon in the center only. Some usually have a tiny crimp mark at one or both poles, and occasionally the marble surface has an orange peel texture to it. They are usually valued from $10 to $20, if Mint.

#254: Akro Agate Company Sparkler

#255: Master Marble Company Sunburst

#256: Foreign "sparkler"

Akro Agate Sparklers

Size	Mint	Near Mint	Good	Collectible
1/2" or less		Too Rare To Value		
9/16" to 11/16"	45.00	20.00	5.00	1.50
23/32" to 25/32"	125.00	60.00	10.00	3.00
7/8" to 1"		Too Rare To Value		
Over 1-1/16"		None Known To Exist		

PELTIER GLASS COMPANY

The Peltier Glass Company was founded in 1886 under the name The Novelty Glass Company by Victor Peltier. The name was changed to the Peltier Glass Company in 1919. The company is located in Ottawa, Illinois, and is still in operation, but no longer produces marbles.

Peltier began making marbles sometime during the early 1920s. Their marbles were marketed under their name and also by M. Gropper & Sons. Peltier produced slags, patches, ribbons and cat's-eyes. Peltier also produced clearies and opaques, but there is no way to identify them as specific to this company.

Peltier slags (#258, #259) are single-stream marbles, as are the slags of other companies. They are a transparent colored base glass with opaque white swirled in. Peltier slags are rarer than the other companies. The most common are brown, blue or green. There are also aqua, purple, red and yellow. The company does not appear to have produced clear or orange slags. Peltier slags are readily identifiable by the very fine feathering pattern produced by the white swirls. This is unique to Peltier. Their slags (as with many Peltier marbles) also tend to have blown out air holes which you usually do not see in the marbles of the other companies.

#258: Peltier Glass Company brown slag

#259: Peltier Glass Company green slag

Peltier Glass Company Slags

Size	Mint	Near Mint	Good	Collectible
1/2" or less		Too Rare To Value		
9/16" to 11/16"	12.50	5.00	1.50	0.50
23/32" to 25/32"	40.00	15.00	7.50	2.50
7/8" to 15/16"		Too Rare To Value		
Over 15/16"		None Known To Exist		

These values are for amber, green or blue. Aqua and purple have a multiple of 1.25x, red has a multiple of 1.5x and yellow has a multiple of 1.75x.

Peltier produced several types of single-stream swirls. These are referred to as "Miller machine" marbles because they were produced on Peltier's first marble machine which was designed by a man named William Miller. These marbles have only one seam. Peltier used another type of machine to produce Rainbos, etc. That machine does not have a name.

An early type of Peltier multicolor swirl was produced by the "Miller machine" (#260). It has a transparent colored base with several opaque colors swirled in, it is much rarer than more common multi-colors where the colors are actually ribbons, not swirls. There are several types of multi-color swirls that have similar coloring to tri-color National Line Rainbos (#261, #262). These are also rare. Another type of "Miller machine" swirl called a Honey Onyx (#263). These are semi-opaque white base with a thin translucent brown patch and a thin translucent green stripe on the marble. They are rare as well.

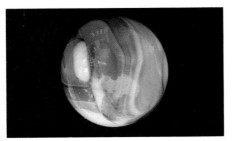

#260: Peltier Glass Company "Miller" multicolor swirl

#262: Peltier Glass Company "Miller" multicolor swirl (Christmas Tree)

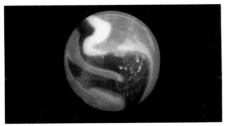

#261: Peltier Glass Company "Miller" multicolor swirl (Liberty)

#263: Peltier Glass Company honey onyx

Peltier Glass Company "Miller machine" Swirls

Size	Mint	Near Mint	Good	Collectible
1/2" or less		Too Rare To Value		
9/16" to 11/16"	75.00	40.00	10.00	5.00
Over 23/32"		Too Rare To Value		
Over 1-1/16"		None Known To Exist		

These values are for "Miller machine" transparent multicolor swirls. Honey onyx are valued about 0.5x. Opaque two- and tri-color swirls are valued at 5x to 7x.

Peltier produced a patch marble which they marketed as the Peerless (#264, #265). The Peerless patches are very collectible today. The marbles are a two-color patch. They are identifiable by the uniqueness of their shades of color and by their design. Peerless patches are the type of marble that Peltier Picture Marbles (comics) are on. The most common color combination is black patch on white, green patch on mustard yellow, transparent green patch on white, red on white, yellow on aqua, or red on aqua. There are other color combinations, but they are rarer. The rarest patch color is called "pearlized" (#266). This is a greenish color that has a satin shimmer or sheen to it. These are very rare. The design of the patch on Peerless patches is unique. The patches of other companies have straight edges. Peltier marbles have patches that have curved or "S" edges. This feature, along with the unique colors, means that Peerless patches are readily identifiable.

#264: Peltier Glass Company Peerless patch (black on white)

#265: Peltier Glass Company Peerless patch (yellow on green)

#266: Peltier Glass Company pearlized Peerless patch (green on blue)

Peltier Glass Company Peerless Patches

Size	Mint	Near Mint	Good	Collectible
1/2" and less	3.00	0.75	0.25	0.10
9/16" to 11/16"	5.00	1.00	0.50	0.10
23/32" to 25/32"	12.50	4.00	1.50	0.50
7/8" to 15/16"	30.00	15.00	8.00	5.00
Over 15/16"		None Known To Exist		

Black aventurine patches have a multiple of 2x to 4x. Rare colors have a multiple of 2x to 10x. Pearlized patches have a multiple of 20x to 30x

One of the most collectible Peltier Glass marbles is the Picture Marble or comic (#269, #270, #271, #272, #273, #274). These are Peltier Peerless patches with a black transfer of one of twelve different King Syndicate comic characters fired on the marble surface. Usually, there is an overglaze of clear glass. The twelve characters (in ascending order of rarity) are Emma, Koko, Bimbo, Andy, Smitty, Skeezix, Annie, Herbie, Sandy, Betty, Moon, Kayo. There are also comic marbles with a transfer of Tom Mix (#267) and with an advertisement for Cotes Master Loaf (#268) on them. These are very rare. The transfers are always on 19/32" to 11/16" Peerless Patches. Each character has a specific marble color combination that is most common to that marble. Rarer color combinations are difficult to find and are valued much higher (#275) Also, there has been a Tom Mix marble reported to have a red transfer, as well as a few transfers of other characters in red or yellow. There has also been a black comic transfer on a 7/8" marble. These are extremely rare, and were probably experimental. A 5/8" Tom Mix marble was sold at auction for $2,650 in October 1993.

#267: Peltier Glass Company Tom Mix comic

#272: Peltier Glass Company comic (Herbie, Sandy)

#268: Peltier Glass Company Cotes comic

#273: Peltier Glass Company comic (Annie, Betty)

#269: Peltier Glass Company comic (Emma, Bimbo)

#274: Peltier Glass Company comic (Kayo, Moon)

#270: Peltier Glass Company comic (Andy, Smitty)

#275: Peltier Glass Company comic (Emma, Sandy, on rare colors)

#271: Peltier Glass Company comic (Koko, Skeezix)

Peltier Glass Company
Picture Marbles ("Comics")

Size	Mint	Near Mint	Good	Collectible
1/2" or less		None Known to Exist		
9/16" to 11/16"	50.00	30.00	15.00	5.00
23/32" to 25/32"		Too Rare To Value		
Over 7/8"		None Known To Exist		

These values are for Emma and Koko. Bimbo, Andy and Smitty have a multiple of 1.5x, Herbie has a multiple of 2x, Skeezix has a multiple of 2x to 2.5x, Annie has a value of 2.5x to 3x, Sandy has a multiple of 3x to 3.5x, Betty has a multiple of 3x to 4x, Moon has a multiple of 4x to 6x, Kayo has a multiple of 6x to 8x. Cotes Master Loaf has a multiple of 15x to 25x. Tom Mix has a multiple of 30x to 45x. Each character has a common color combination on the marble. Rarer marble color combinations have additional multiples.

The majority of collectible Peltier Glass Company marbles are ribboned type. The most collectible of these are the National Line Rainbo. These marbles are an opaque base color with four to eight ribbons in the surface. The tri-colors can be distinguished from "Miller Machine" marbles because they have two seams on them. Also, the ribbons are usually translucent to transparent on the tri-color National Line Rainbos, and opaque on the "Miller Machine" tri-colors.

If the ribbons are all the same color, then the marble is referred to as a two-color National Line Rainbo. The base color can be either opaque white or an opaque color. Some of the color combinations have inspired imaginative names among collectors. Zebras are black ribbon on white base (#276), Blue Zebras are blue ribbon on white base (#277), Bumblebee is black ribbon on yellow base (#278), Blue Bee is blue aventurine on yellow base, Cub Scout is yellow ribbon on blue base (#279), Wasp is black ribbon on red base (#280), Blue Wasp is blue ribbon on red base, Tiger is black ribbon on orange base (#281), Blue Tiger is blue ribbon on orange base. Chocolate Cow is black ribbon on brown base. National Line Rainbos with ribbons of two different colors are called Tri-color National Line Rainbos. They have also inspired a series of imaginative names. Ketchup & Mustard (#282) is opaque white base with red and yellow ribbons, Christmas Tree (#283) is opaque white base with red and green ribbons, Liberty (#284) is opaque white base with red and blue ribbons. Gray-Coat is opaque white base with red and gray ribbons. Rebel (#285) is an opaque white or yellow base with black and red ribbons. Golden Rebel is opaque yellow base with red and black ribbons (#286). Superman (#287) is opaque light blue base with yellow and red ribbons. Flaming Dragon is red and yellow on green base. Blue Galaxy is red or yellow and aventurine black on light blue opaque base. Hybrid examples also exist. A 27/32" Golden Rebel was sold for $2,993 in a March 1998 auction.

#276: Peltier Glass Company National Line Rainbo (Zebra)

#277: Peltier Glass Company National Line Rainbo (Blue Zebra)

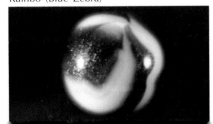

#278: Peltier Glass Company National Line
Rainbo (Bumblebee)

#283: Peltier Glass Company National Line
Rainbo (Christmas Tree)

#279: Peltier Glass Company National Line
Rainbo (Cub Scout)

#284: Peltier Glass Company National Line
Rainbo (Liberty)

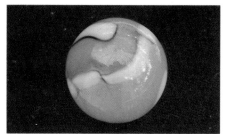

#280: Peltier Glass Company National Line
Rainbo (Wasp)

#285: Peltier Glass Company National Line
Rainbo (Rebel)

#281: Peltier Glass Company National Line
Rainbo (Tiger)

#282: Peltier Glass Company National Line
Rainbo (Ketchup & Mustard)

#286: Peltier Glass Company National Line
Rainbo (Golden Rebel)

#287: Peltier Glass Company National Line
Rainbo (Superman)

Peltier Glass Company
National Line Rainbos

Size	Mint	Near Mint	Good	Collectible
1/2" or less	15.00	4.00	1.50	0.25
9/16" to 11/16"	15.00	5.00	1.00	1.00
23/32" to 25/32"	35.00	12.50	7.50	2.00
7/8" to 15/16"	175.00	75.00	25.00	15.00
Over 15/16"		Too Rare To Value		

These values are for white-base, two-color National Line Rainbos. Two-color color-base National Line Rainbos have a multiple of 1.5x to 3x. Bumblebees, wasps, and tigers have a multiple of 3x to 5x. Blue aventurine have a multiple of 5x to 10x. Ketchup & Mustard, Christmas Tree, Liberty and white-base Rebels without aventurine have a multiple of 8x to 12x. White-base Rebels with aventurine have a multiple of 10x to 15x. Gray-coats have a multiple of about 12x to 18x. Supermen have a multiple of 15x to 25x. Golden Rebels have a multiple of 20x to 30x. Flaming Dragons and Blue Galaxies have a multiple of 25x to 50x. Hybrids have a multiple of 15x to 25x. Currently, there is no real difference in value between Type I and Type II National Line Rainbos.

The more common ribboned Peltier marble is the Rainbo. These are a more recent marble than the National Line Rainbo. As with the National Line Rainbo, they are a two seam design. The base glass can be a variety of opaque or transparent colors, depending on the particular type of Rainbo, and they all have a ribbon or pair of ribbons encircling the equator of the marble. There is a basic difference between a National Line Rainbo and a Rainbo. In a National Line Rainbo, the ribbons lay just on and below the surface of the marble. This is easily seen on a National Line Rainbo that has chips on the ribbons. In a Rainbo, the ribbons go into the marble, towards the core.

Opaque base with a pair of colored ribbons encircling the equator are called Rainbos (#288). Translucent base with a pair of colored ribbons encircling the equator are called Acme Realers (#289). An opalescent base with a pair of red ribbons encircling the equator are called Bloodie (#290). A bubble-filled transparent clear base with a red and white, orange and white, or yellow and white pair of ribbons encircling the equator are called Sunsets (#291). A transparent dark base with a yellow and white ribbon brushed on the equator of the marble is a Champion Jr (#292). An opaque colored base (#293) or transparent colored base (#294) with a pair of different colored ribbons encircling the equator are called Tri-colors. Transparent clear with ribbons of two or three different colors are called Clear Rainbos (#295). There are also Rainbos with opaque white base and two different colors in the ribbons (similar to tri-color National Line Rainbos).

Many variations on the above basic marbles are turning up all the time, although Rainbos do not seem to have quite the variety of corkscrews. Some Rainbos have been found with six ribbons instead of four, and Rainbos with different colors on either side. The values for these variations were still volatile at the time this guide was revised.

A number of different variations on National Line Rainbo designs and Rainbo designs have been found. Whether this indicates different machinery or just different operation of the same machine, we don't know. Discussions among collectors are just beginning to result in classifications of types. At the time this book went to press, the following variations had been identified:

Miller machine - Very heavily swirled. May have more than six separate ribbons. One tiny seam.

NLR Type I - Four to eight ribbons, heavily swirled. Two seams, although they may be very close to each other on the marble surface.

NLR Type II - Four to eight ribbons. Very straight lines (running along the equatorial axis). There may or may not be ribbons near the equator. Two very distinct seams at opposite sides of the marble.

NLR Type III - Four ribbon only. Two seams. Two ribbons with a seam in the middle form on side of the marble, the other two ribbons with seam in the middle are on the other side. Set at 90 degree angle to each other (similar to a universal joint on a car or truck).

NLR Type IV - Four ribbon only. Broken corkscrew pattern (spiral from one end of the marble to the other). Two seams, although there may appear to be more because of the amount of swirling on the marble surface.

NLR Type V - Four ribbons only. Two seams. Two equatorial ribbons form a band around the equator. One patch on top, one on the bottom.

Rainbo Type I - Same as NLR Type V, but a Rainbo.

Rainbo Type II - Six ribbon Rainbo. Four ribbons on the equator form two bands. Sometimes color bleeds to the surface between the bands. A patch at either pole.

Rainbo Type III - Four ribbon Rainbo. Typical Rainbo with four ribbons on the equator forming two bands. Sometime color bleeds to the surface between bands.

The ribbons on National Line Rainbos only lay on the surface or go just under the surface. The ribbons on Rainbos go much farther into the marble, sometimes all the way to the center.

#288: Peltier Glass Company Rainbo

#289: Peltier Glass Company Rainbo (Acme Realer)

#291: Peltier Glass Company Rainbo (Sunset)

#290: Peltier Glass Company Rainbo (Bloodie)

#292: Peltier Glass Company Rainbo (Champion Jr.)

#293: Peltier Glass Company Rainbo (Tri-color)

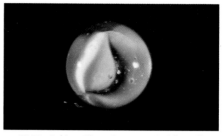

#295: Peltier Glass Company Rainbo (Clear Rainbo)

#294: Peltier Glass Company Rainbo (Tri-color)

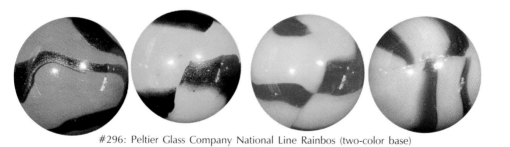

#296: Peltier Glass Company National Line Rainbos (two-color base)

Peltier Glass Company Rainbos

Size	Mint	Near Mint	Good	Collectible
1/2" or less	0.50	0.10	0.01	N/V
9/16" to 11/16"	0.50	0.10	0.01	N/V
23/32" to 25/32"	1.00	0.25	0.10	0.01
7/8" to 15/16"	5.00	1.50	0.50	0.10
31/32" to 1"	7.50	2.00	0.75	0.25
Over 1-1/16"		None Known to Exist		

These are values for Type II Rainbos, Acme Realers and Tri-colors. Bloodies have a multiple of 1.5x to 3x. Sunsets have a multiple of 1.5x to 2x. Champion Jrs have a multiple of 2x. Clear rainbos have a multiple of 40x to 50x. Other type, rare designs or color combinations have additional multiples.

Peltier also produced a type of cat's-eye. The marble consists of a single-vaned opaque color in transparent clear glass. They are referred to as Bananas because the shape of the vane looks like a banana (#297). These marbles are fairly common, although not as common as other American or foreign cat's-eyes. The most common color for the vane is yellow, red, blue, green or white. Other colors as well as colored baseglass, are less common (#298). There is also a type of Peltier cat's-eye that is similar to the Banana. These were only produced for a short period of time. They are a transparent dark amber base with a flat wide white vane in the middle. They are sometimes referred to by marble collectors as a Peltier Root Beer Float (#299) and have only been found in the 11/16" to 7/8" size. They were a limited run.

#299: Peltier Glass Company Root Beer Float

#297: Peltier Glass Company Banana

#298: Peltier Glass Company Banana (rare color, lavender)

Peltier Glass Company Cat's-eyes

Size	Mint	Near Mint	Good	Collectible
1/2" or less		Too Rare To Value		
9/16" to 11/16"	0.50	0.10	0.01	N/V
23/32" to 25/32"	1.00	0.25	0.10	0.01
7/8" to 15/16"	2.00	0.50	0.25	0.10
31/32" to 1"	5.00	2.00	0.75	0.25
Over 1-1/16"		None Known To Exist		

These are values for Bananas with common color vanes. Less common colors can have multiples of 1.5x to 20x. Root Beer Floats have a multiple of 50x to 100x.

THE MASTER MARBLE COMPANY/ THE MASTER GLASS COMPANY

The Master Marble Company was founded in 1930 by four former employees of the Akro Agate Company. The company closed in 1941 and the machinery was purchased by one of the former owners who formed The Master Glass Company. Master Glass closed in 1973.

The Master Marble Company used machinery which was similar to Akro Agate's, but most notably, did not include the Freese improvement which offset the rollers. This means that Master marbles have a crimp or feathering mark at either pole. Also, due to the design of the machinery, Master marbles have a unique pattern at either end. At either end you can see a small "V" of the color on one side of the marble indenting into the color on the other side.

The most collectible Master marble is the Sunburst, and a related marble called the Tiger-Eye. The Sunburst (#300) was an attempt to duplicate handmade onion-skins. The marble is a transparent clear base with filaments and strands of various colors running from pole to pole and completely filling the marble. Some Sunbursts have clear patches or areas in them (#301). A Tiger-Eye (#302) is a Sunburst that is almost completely clear. It has filaments and strands forming a wide, flat ribbon in the center of the marble. They are rarer than Sunbursts. The colors are usually orange, white and black in a transparent clear base.

#300: Master Marble
Company Sunburst (opaque)

#301: Master Marble
Company Sunburst (clear)

#302: Master Marble
Company Tiger Eye

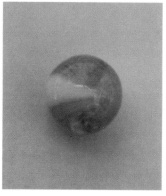

Master Marble Company Sunbursts

Size	Mint	Near Mint	Good	Collectible
9/16" to 11/16"	7.50	3.00	1.00	0.10
23/32" to 25/32"	15.00	5.00	2.00	0.25
Over 7/8"		None Known to Exist		

These values are for Sunbursts of average coloring. Marbles with bright colors or clear patches have multiples of 1.25x to 3x. Tiger-Eyes have multiples of 6x to 8x.

Master Marble also made some patch marbles that are collectible. These patches were marketed under a variety of names, including Meteor (#303) (wispy translucent patch on opaque base), Comet (#304) (opaque patch on opaque base) and Cloudy (#305) (translucent patch on translucent base). The Master Marble patches are identifiable by a "V" or "U" pattern (#305) and feathering seen at each pole. The patches were made in a variety of patterns, including two-color opaque, two-color translucent, and opaque with a second color brushed on. Master Marbles' colors are relatively unique, although generally duller than Akro's.

#303: Master Marble Company patch (Meteor)

#304: Master Marble Company patch (Comet)

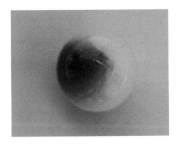

#305: Master Marble Company patch

Master Marble Company Patches

Size	Mint	Near Mint	Good	Collectible
1/2" or less		Too Rare To Value		
9/16" to 11/16"	1.00	0.10	0.01	N/V
23/32" to 25/32"	2.00	0.25	0.10	0.01
Over 7/8"		None Known To Exist		

Master Marble and Master Glass made a variety of clearies, opaques and cat's-eyes (Master Glass only). Master clearies and opaques all have the typical "V" or "U" pattern at either end. Master cat's-eyes are typically single color translucent three vane variety in transparent clear glass.

Alley Companies

Lawrence Alley operated factories in at least four different locations in West Virginia (Paden City, Sistersville, Pennsboro and St. Mary's) between 1929 and 1949. He also may have operated a plant in Salem, West Virginia. In 1949, he sold the St. Mary's plant to Berry Pink and Sellers Peltier, and they changed the company name to Marble King. As well as moving around, the company changed its name several times during its existence. Variously, it was known as Alley Agate Company, Lawrence Glass Novelty Company, and Alley Glass Manufacturing Company. Most Alley marbles were distributed by J. E. Pressman.

Alley produced a large variety of transparent, translucent and opaque swirls (#489), as well as chinese checkers. Many of the swirls have "flame"designs to them (#488). Some collectors believe since Alley began operations very soon after Christensen Agate ceased operations, that the Christensen Agate machinery and/or Christensen Agate workers ended up at Alley. No corroborating evidence has turned up yet in research to support this hypothesis, but it is an intriguing possibility.

Alley produced a large variety of two and three color swirls (#476), as well as single color opaques and clearies. Sizes ranged from 3/8" to about an inch. More research is needed in order to positively identify the unique marbles that Alley made. It is known that Alley produced marbles using metallic color, as well as a type of oxblood. As mentioned above, many of the swirls feature flame patterns reminiscent of Christensen Agate.

Alley Agate swirls range in value from $0.25 to $20.00 each, depending on the number of colors and quality of the design. The 3/8" marbles are rare and are valued at $20 to $40 each.

#476: Alley Agate Company

#488. Alley Agate Company swirl

#489. Alley Agate Company swirl

MARBLE KING, INC.

Marble King was started in 1949 by Berry Pink and Sellers Peltier in St. Mary's, West Virginia. It was moved to Paden City, West Virginia, in 1958 after a fire destroyed the original plant. The machinery was purchased from the Alley Glass Company. Berry Pink had also been jobbing marbles since the 1920s under the trade name "Berry Pink, Inc."

Marble King produced ribboned, patch & ribboned, cat's-eye, and swirl marbles. Most are collectible today.

Patch & ribbon marbles have a patch on one pole, a ribbon of a second color encircling the marble, a ribbon of the same color as the top patch encircling the marble and finally a patch of the second color on the bottom pole. The marbles have two seams. They are made using a veneering method which puts a thin layer of the colored glass on a base of white glass. These marbles were marketed under the name "Rainbows."

The most common Rainbow is white alternating with another color (#306). The second color is usually red, blue, brown or green. There are Rainbows that are white with a color ribbon and patch consisting of two or three different colors (#307). These are rarer. The most collectible Rainbows are two different alternating colors (not white). These have descriptive names that have been given to them by collectors. In ascending order of rarity: Bumblebee (yellow & black) (#308), Wasp (red & black) (#309), Cub Scout (blue & yellow) (#310), Girl Scout (green & yellow) (#311), Tiger (orange & yellow) (#312), Ruby Bee (red and yellow), Spiderman (red & blue) (#313), Green Hornet (green & black) (#314), Watermelon (red & green) (#315), Dragonfly (green and blue). There are also hybrid examples that are either a patch (#316) or consist of three or four colors (#317). These are very rare. Spidermen, Green Hornets, Watermelons and Dragonflies have only been found in the 5/8" size. Girl Scouts and Tigers have only been found up to 3/4". Larger examples (up to 1") exist of the other types.

Some experimental Marble King Rainbows have surfaced that have a completely transparent clear base with one color patch and ribbonned on the surface. These are very rare and difficult to value.

Another collectible Marble King marble is the Rainbow Red. This is a white base marble with an equatorial ribbon of red and a second equatorial ribbon of a different color, rather than a patch.

There are several types of new marbles being produced, or that have been recently produced, that are very similar to vintage Rainbows in terms of color and pattern. These include Rainbow-looking marbles that have a translucent base, Rainbow-looking marbles that are missing the patch but have the equatorial ribbon, and Rainbow-looking marbles where the two colors are blended together in thin strands or bands. None of these have much value.

The past several years have seen a tremendous expansion in the types and color combinations of Marble King marbles that have been found. Much of this has been fueled by a number of dig sites in the West Virginia area, as well as a well-publicized theft from the plant archives. Aside from the influx of "blended" Marble Kings and Berry Pinks into the marketplace, there has been a flood of white based "hybrid" Rainbows in a variety of color combinations that rivals that found in Akro corkscrews. Many of these "hybrids" have been dug at former plant sites. The total supply of these is unknown, and prices are very volatile at the time of this writing.

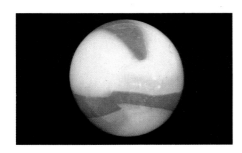

#306: Marble King Inc. Rainbow (two-color, white base)

#307: Marble King Inc. Rainbow (multi-color, white base)

#308: Marble King Inc. Rainbow (bumblebee)

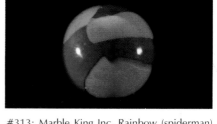

#313: Marble King Inc. Rainbow (spiderman)

#309: Marble King Inc. Rainbow (wasp)

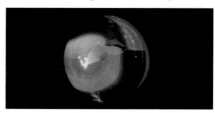

#314: Marble King Inc. Rainbow (green hornet)

#310: Marble King Inc. Rainbow (cub scout)

#315: Marble King Inc. Rainbow (watermelon)

#311: Marble King Inc. Rainbow (girl scout)

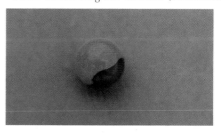

#316: Marble King Inc. Rainbow (patch, spiderman)

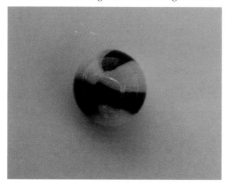

#312: Marble King Inc. Rainbow (tiger)

#317: Marble King Inc. Rainbow (hybrid, spiderman/watermelon)

Marble King Inc. Rainbows

Size	Mint	Near Mint	Good	Collectible
1/2" or less		None Known To Exist		
9/16" to 11/16"	1.00	0.25	0.05	0.01
23/32" to 25/32"	7.50	5.00	3.00	0.50
7/8" to 15/16"	20.00	12.50	4.00	1.50
31/32" to 1"	25.00	15.00	6.00	2.50
Over 1-1/16"		None Known To Exist		

These values are for Bumblebees. White-base two-color have a multiple of 0.05x, white-base multicolor have a multiple of 0.10x to 2x, depending on colors. Wasps have a multiple of 2.5x, Cub Scouts have a multiple of 5x, Girl Scouts have a multiple of 7x, Tigers have a multiple of 15X to 20x. Spidermen and Green Hornets have a multiple of 150x to 500x and Watermelons have a multiple of 200x to 600x. Dragonflies have a multiple of 400x to 600x. Rainbow Reds have a multiple of 0.75x to 1x.

Ravenswood Novelty Works

The Ravenswood Novelty Works began operations during 1931 or 1932, under the guidance of John Turnbull. Operations continued until about 1954 or 1955, when Paul Cox, the son-in-law of Turnbull who ran the company after the deaths of Turnbull and his wife, decided to close the company. It has been reported that as late as 1959, Ravenswood was making industrial marbles, which it supplied to Krylon Paint for their aerosol cans (Ravenswood was Krylon's major supplier), but these may have been marbles bought from Vitro Agate Company. Ravenswood's marble machines were sold to Bogard Glass Company and Champion Agate Company after it ceased production

Ravenswood made transparent and opaque swirls (#318, #319,#320, #321, #323). There is also strong evidence to suggest that they made the 1" Buddy marbles (#322) and did not buy them from Master Glass as had been previously believed. Typically, marbles with an opaque base will be swirled with translucent or transparent, and those with a transparent base will be swirled with opaque swirls. Many transparent swirls contain one color in addition to wispy white swirls. Marbles are predominately 9/16" to 5/8", except for the 1" marbles mentioned above.Common base colors include white, light green, green, light blue, yellow, light purple, and cream. Brown is the rarest. Swirls can contain two, three or four colors. Ravenswood swirls are very unique in terms of coloring and design. Many of the swirl designs are similar to Christensen Agate and Alley Agate. The value of Ravenswood 9/16" to 5/8" swirls ranges from $0.25 to $25 depending on pattern, colors and number of colors. The 1" swirls generally were only made in two-color patterns. They are valued at $10-$15

#318. Ravenswood Company swirl

#319. Ravenswood Company swirl

#320. Ravenswood Company swirl

#321. Ravenswood Company swirl

#322: Ravenswood Novelty Works
multicolor swirl

Ravenswood Novelty Works Swirls

Size	Mint	Near Mint	Good	Collectible
9/16" to 5/8"	3.00	0.50	0.05	0.01
11/16" to 23/32"	5.00	2.00	0.50	0.10
3/4" to 7/8"	8.00	3.00	1.00	0.25
15/16" to 1"	10.00	4.50	1.50	0.50
Over 1"		None Known To Exist		

These values are for average white-base two-color examples. Brighter colors have a multiple of 1.25x to 3x higher. Three-color examples have a multiple of 2x to 4x higher. Flame-types have a multiple of 1.5x to 3x higher than a similarly colored example.

VITRO AGATE COMPANIES

The Vitro Agate Company began operations in 1932 in Parkersburg, West Virginia. It was acquired in 1969 by The Gladding Corporation, which changed the name to Gladding-Vitro Agate Company. In 1982, Gladding-Vitro was purchased by Paris Manufacturing Company, which changed the name back to Vitro Agate. In 1987, it was purchased by Viking Rope Company which retained the name, but moved the company to Anacortes, Washington. The company ceased operations in 1993 and the machinery and name were purchased by JABO, Inc. sometime after that. It then became JABO-Vitro Agate Company.

Early Vitro Agate marbles are the brushed variety. This is the type that has a thin layer of colored glass brushed on a base color. There are also a few veneered varieties, but these manufactured later on.

More recently, Vitro Agate also made some two-seam marbles that are similar to Marble King Rainbows. Marble King appears to have had machinery that produced at least three types of seam marks. One type of machine produced a seam on the other side of the equator that was straight and at a perpendicular angle to the poles. A second type of seam has a "U" shape on either side of the equator. However, unlike Master Marbles that have the two "U"s going in the same direction around the marble, Marble King "U"s point towards each other. This seam design appears to be from an earlier machine and only shows up on Marble King marbles. A third seam type produces a seam on either side of the equator. One seam is straight and the other is "U" shaped. This seam type shows up on Marble King and Vitro Agate marbles.

Vitro Agate also appears to have produced several types of seam marks. One type of machine produced a seam on either side of the equator that are straight and perpendicular to the poles, but that have a crimp or ridge to them (that is you can feel it with your finger). Another type of machine produced a seam on either side of the equator. One seam is straight and the other is "U" shaped. This seam type is found on Marble King marbles too.

Vitro also produced a number of two seam multicolor patch marbles. Many of these have clear and wispy white as one of the colors. When viewed ninety degrees around the marble from a seam, many have a stylized "V" pattern to them.

A Victory (#324) is a transparent clear base with an opaque color patch brushed on about a quarter of the surface. The patch is purple, green, yellow, blue or red. The Conqueror (#325) is more common than the Victory. It is a transparent clear base with the same type of patch as the Victory. However, the remainder of the marble is brushed with opaque white. These marbles are usually found in 5/8", but examples up to 15/16" are known to exist. There are two other marbles, similar to a Conqueror. One looks just like a Conqueror, but most of the interior of the marble is filled with translucent white filaments (occasionally the marble is opalescent) (#326). These are often referred to as "phantom conquerors." They are much more common than the Conqueror and are not collectible at this time. The other type is very similar to a Conqueror, but has a brushed white that is more off-white than a Conqueror and a colored patch that is not as bright (#331). These are beginning to become collectible and in the 5/8" size are valued at $5 to $10 each.

#324: Vitro Agate Company Victory

#325: Vitro Agate Company Conqueror

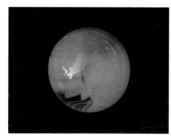

#326: Vitro Agate Company patched ("Phantom" Conqueror)

Vitro Agate Company Victory & Conqueror

Size	Mint	Near Mint	Good	Collectible
1/2" or less		None Known To Exist		
9/16" to 11/16"	1.00	0.01	N/V	N/V
23/32" to 7/8"	7.50	0.50	0.10	0.01
15/16" to 1"	12.50	1.50	0.25	0.10
Over 1-1/16"		None Known To Exist		

These values are for Victories. Conquerors have multiples of 0.33x to 0.5x.

Another type of Vitro Agate that has recently become collectible were marketed as Blackies and Whities (#327). Blackies are opaque black with a white or colored band around the equator. Whities are opaque white with a color band around the equator. A slightly more recent Vitro-Agate are the All-Reds (#328, #329). All-Reds come in two varieties. The older variety is an opaque white base with a color patch on one pole and a different color on the other. There is a black line encircling the red patch. The other type of All-Red, which is newer, has a color patch on one pole and a different color patch on the other. There is no black line on this one. The Blackies and All-Reds are valued at about $0.03 to $0.05 each for the 5/8" size, up to about $0.25 each for the 15/16" size. Whities and Blackies have only been found in 5/8" and are valued at $2.00-$3.00 each.

Vitro Agate also produced another type of brushed opaque marble called the "Parrot" (#330), that has recently become collectible. This is a white base marble that has four or more patches of color on it. The patches can be blue, purple, black, red, yellow and aventurine green. I have seen these marbles in the 3/4" to 1" size. They are valued about $35 if Mint. The less white showing, the higher the value.

Vitro Parrots, as well as other Vitro swirls sometimes have a "V" pattern in the glass. This was intentional. A good "V" can significantly increase the value of the marble (#333).

Vitro Agate made a wide variety of other transparent and opaque marbles, as well as cat's-eyes. Almost all have little value today. However, there are several that collectors are beginning to look for. The Vitro Agate multi-color patch (#332) is a transparent clear base marble with four different colored patches brushed on the surface. They are valued about $0.10, if Mint. If one of the patches is Vitro "oxblood" the value is about $25.00. Vitro Agate also produced some cat's-eyes that are beginning to be collected. Vitro Agate cat's-eyes are either a four or five wavy vane type. Gladding-Vitro cat's-eyes are a five to eight strand cage style. Some cage styles can be found in aqua glass (#334). These are the most valuable, ranging from $10 to $50. There are some Vitro Agate vane-style cat's-eyes that have two or more colors on each vane. These are referred to as hybrids (#335), although they seem to be too common to have been an accident. They are generally valued at around $1.

#327: Vitro Agate Company Whitie

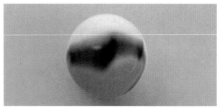

#328: Vitro Agate Company All-Red (old style)

#329: Vitro Agate Company All-Red (new style)

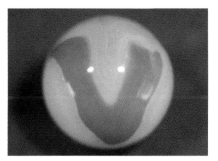

#330: Vitro Agate Company parrot

#331: Vitro Agate Company "oxblood"

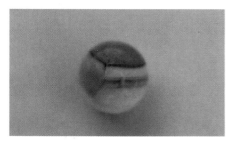
#332: Vitro Agate Company Tigereye

#334: Gladding-Vitro Inc. cats-eye

#333: Vitro Agate Company "V" patch

#335. Vitro Agate Company hybrid catseye

Champion Agate Company

The Champion Agate Company began operations in Pennsboro West Virginia in 1938. It was founded by Yucca Jones and Ralph Michels. Ownership passed over time through several members of the Michels family.

The first marbles the company produced were clearies and Chinese checkers. Very soon after, the company moved into opaque swirls, transparent swirls and opaque patches. In the mid-1970s the company ceased production of all swirls and patches and concentrated on Chinese checkers. However, from time to time Champion would do limited production runs of swirls. This began with the red, white, and blue swirl in 1976 that was the companies contribution to the "Bicentennial Special Pack", a package of marbles containing examples from most of the companies still operating at that time.

#336: Champion Agate
Company swirl

#337. Champion Agate Company
furnace scraping marble

#338: Champion Agate
Company new "Old-Fashioned"

Champion revived two old styles in 1983 and 1984, the "Whirlwind" and "Old Fashioned". **(#338)** Other types appeared insubsequent years, perhaps most prominently the "Furnace Scraping" **(#337)** marbles of 1994.

Most Champion Agate opaque swirls are opaque white-based. On these marbles there is usually only one color in addition to the white, with swirl patterns forming ribbons that fill little of the base glass, as opposed to the swirls by many other companies that cover the majority of the white. During the 1950s, Champion began production of transparent and translucent base swirls. Many of Champions swirls are difficult to distinguish from those made by other West Virginia companies during that time. Perhaps the easiest to identify are the coral and green swirls.

Most Champion Agate marbles are about 5/8", although some o fthe 1970s New Old Fashioneds are a larger size. Common Champion Agate swirls are valued in the $0.10 to $5.00 depending on the coloring and detail of design (as well as the certainty that the seller has that the marble is in fact Champion Agate). The coral and green swirls are valued at $5-$12.50, depending on the vibrancy and design of the marble. Bicentennial swirls are valued at about $2.50. New Old Fashioned and Whirlwind swirls are valued at $1.00 to $5.00. Furnace scraping marbles are valued at $1.00 to $100.00, depending on color and presence of annealing fractures.

Alox Manufacturing Company

The Alox Manufacturing Company began operations in 1919 in St. Louis, Missouri. It was founded by John Frier. It distributed the marbles of other companies until the early 1930s, at which point Alox began producing their own marbles. Production ceased during World War II, then began again for a few years. The company distributed marbles until the early 1960s. The company itself was operational until 1989, however it did not sell marbles during its final quarter century of existence.

Alox produced chinese checkers and opaque and transparent swirls. The swirls were sold in their "Three-in-a-Row Tit-Tat-Toe" boxes (valued at $25-$35) and in mesh

bags (valued at $20-$35). Most of the swirls are indistinguishable from those made by the other manufacturers of the time. However, some of the transparent swirls are fairly unique. These tend to have clear, green or blue base with thick opaque white swirls (#339). The swirls are sized about 5/8" and are valued at $0.10 to $1.00.

#339. Alox Agate Company swirl

Heaton Agate Company

The Heaton Agate Company began operations in 1946 or 1947 in Pennsboro, West Virginia. It was originally run by Bill Heaton and Oris Hanlon. Hanlon left the company in 1947 to found the Cairo Novelty Company. Until the early 1960s, the company produced a variety of opaque swirls and transparent swirls, as well as cat's-eye and chinese checkers. During the 1960s, production of swirls ceased and the company restricted itself to producing cat's-eyes and industrial marbles.

Heaton swirls are white, cream, green or blue base (#477). The cream base usually has green swirls, the green base has red swirls and the blue base has red or green swirls. Heaton cat's-eyes are four-vane, usually with transparent pale white/blue, dark blue or light green vanes. Marbles are about 5/8". The swirls are valued at $0.10 to $1.00, cat's-eyes are valued at $0.05 to $0.10.

#477: Heaton Agate Company   #478: JABO - Vitro Agate Company

C.E. Bogard & Sons Company, Bogard Company

C.E. Bogard bought The Heaton Agate Company in 1971 and changed it's name to the C.E. Bogard & Sons Company. In 1983 the company name was changed to The Bogard Company by Clayton Bogard's son, Jack. Bogard produced a variety of cat's-eyes, clearies and opaques. According to Jack Bogard, the company also produced an experimental marble (transparent clear base with interior green wisps) that can be found in the Mountaineer blister packs that the company marketed. Bogard catseyes are similar to Heaton catseyes, but not as well formed (#401). It is difficult to identify Bogard marbles if not in their original packaging. Bogard marbles are about 5/8". The cat's-eyes are valued atabout $0.10 to $0.25, the experimental green wisps are valued at about $0.25 to$1.00. The Mountaineer blister pack is valued at $15.00 to $20.00.

JABO, Inc.

JABO, Inc. was organized in 1987 by Jack Bogard, DaveMcCullough (who had spent many years at Champion Agate) and Joanne Argabrite. The machinery was moved to Reno Ohio. The company produced industrial marbles, mainly opaques. However, Dave McCullough would produce three or four limited runs each year of "Classics" in sizes form 5/8" to 1". Each run was different from the previous run, and the marbles unlike those made by any other company. Many fluoresce. They contain many innovative colors and were produced in short runs. JABO Classics are valued in the $0.50 to $5.00 range.

Jabo-Vitro Agate Company

In early 1996, JABO Inc. bought the Vitro Agate Company, moving the equipment from Anacortes Washington to Reno Ohio. Jabo-Vitro Agate Company now produces a wide range of clearie, oily, chinese checker and swirls (#490), as well as limited runs of their Classics. Marbles range in size from 1/2" to1".

Jabo-Vitro swirls often have tiny white hit marks on the surface. This is a result of the soft glass being bruised as the marbles fall down the chutes from the machine into the collection bins. Many of the swirl patterns are similar to early Vitro Agate marbles, and some have poor "turkey-heads" on them. Jabo-Vitro swirls can often be identified from the swirls of other companies not only by these characteristics but by the glass.

Quite often, the glass is fluorescent and may glow either orange or yellow. The colors, too, are distinctive, and are usually not opaque but rather are transparent or translucent. Sometimes the glass will have a milky or cloudy appearance. The colors swirl deeply inside the base glass and also appear to be brushed on the surface. Common swirls are valued at $0.01 to $0.10. Classics are valued at $0.50 to $2.00.

#490. Jabo-Vitro Agate Company Classics

Jackson Marble Company

Carol Jackson founded The Jackson Marble Company about 1945, near Pennsboro, West Virginia. He had previously been a machine operator at Champion Agate Company. The company did not exist for very long and is generally believed to have produced only about two boxcars full of marbles.

Most of the information we have about Jackson marbles comes from recent digs in the area of the factory site. Jackson marbles often have dull, transparent colors, although they can exhibit attractive combinations and swirl patterns (**#491**). The marbles are about 5/8″ and are valued at $0.50 to $5.00.

#491. Jackson Marble Company swirl

Davis Marble Works

Wilson Davis founded The Davis Marble Works in 1947, in Pennsboro, West Virginia. He was a World War II veteran and purchased an old Alley Agate marble making machine from Corning Glass. Like Jackson Marble Company, Davis Marble Works did not survive forlong. It is estimated that relatively few marbles were produced.

Most of the information we have about Davis marbles comes from recent digs in the area of the factory site. Davis produced mostly transparent swirls, some with distinct shades (#492). They are about 5/8″ and are valued at $0.50 to $5.00

#492. Davis Marble Works swirl

Playrite Marble and Novelty Company

Playrite Marble and Novelty Company operated from later 1945 until late 1947. It was located in Lamberton (now Ellenboro) on a lot that is now used by Mid-Atlantic for their marble factory outlet. The owners were Jesse Krupp, Andy Long and Lawrence Jones. In early 1946, C.A. Wilson and Joseph Wilson purchased stock in the company.

Playrite produced swirl type marbles (#493). When the company closed, they need bags for the leftover marbles. They acquired a number of unused Jackson Marble Company mesh bags with Jackson header labels and filled those with Playrite marbles.

#493. Playrite Marble Company swirl

(Thanks to Mary Jane Wilson for the above information).

CAIRO NOVELTY COMPANY

The Cairo Novelty Company began operations in 1948 in Cairo, West Virginia. With the financial backing of two local merchants (John Sandy and Dennis Farley), it had been formed late in the prior year by Oris Hanlon, who had left Heaton Agate Company. The company had only one marble machine, but a design innovation by Hanlon (which is patented) allowed it to produce marbles at a fifty percent faster rate than any other machine at the time. The company produced a wide variety of swirls (#479) from pee-wee size to 3/4". Many of these marbles fluoresce. Their major account was Woolworth's, and they packaged mesh bags with the Woolworth's label on them. Cairo also marketed marbles in boxes with their own name. Both of these original packages are hard to find. The company also produced and market a game called "Trap the Fox" in the late 1940s. The game included black and white swirls (the hounds) and an opaque marble (the fox). A flash flood in 1950 seriously curtailed operations, but Cairo was able to produce marbles until 1953. Cairo Swirls are valued at $0.50 to $10.00.

#479: Cairo Novelty Company

Vacor de Mexico

Vacor de Mexico began operations in Guadalajara, Mexico, about 1930. It originally produced clay marbles, but by the mid-1930s was producing glass marbles. They are today the largest marble producer in the world, accounting for over 90% of the world marble production, by some accounts.

Little is known about marbles produced by Vacor de Mexico before the early 1980s. During the past few decades, the company has taken a more serious approach to marketing their marbles, assigning a bewildering array of names to them. These include Pirate, Galaxy, Meteor, Galactica, Silver, Agate, Dalmation, Destroyer, Spaghetti, to name but a few (#340, #341).

Vacor marbles often have an oily or iridescent sheen to them. The glass also tends to have ripples and creases in the surface.

Vacor de Mexico marbles range from 9/16" to over 1". They are valued from $0.10 to $5.00 or more.

#340: Vacor de Mexico

#341. Vacor de Mexico

EUROPEAN MACHINE-MADE MARBLES

Machine-made marbles that were manufactured in Europe have begun to be identified by collectors. There are several types of marbles that have been positively identified as coming from Europe. The first is the "foreign sparkler." These have appeared in two versions. The faded pastel color (#256), and a more colorful version (#480). The faded pastel type appears to be of more recent vintage than the brighter type, and appears to have been made by a different manufacturer. The "bright" type has a thin vane in the center with assorted bright colors on it. The poles exhibit the "V" or "U" pattern similar to Master Marbles. I have only seen it in sizes between 19/32" and 3/4". They are valued at $10 to $25, if Mint. I believe that these marbles are from the 1940s or 1950s. Aside from loose examples, I have seen two examples, each embedded an a bar of soap shaped like a little girl. One of the bars of soap was in a box indicating it had been manufactured in France. The "faded pastel" type has a wide vane that fills the marble. The surface has an "orange peel" texture and usually has creases at the seam lines. This marble is probably Vacor de Mexico. They are usually found about 1" in diameter and are valued at about $10, if Mint.

Another type of European marble is a Wire Pull (#481). These have been found in a multitude of sizes, base colors and wire colors. It is almost certain that they were manufactured in Germany, possibly in the 1960s. If Mint, they range in value from $1 to $25 or more (depending on the brightness of the color and the intricacy of the wire).

A marble referred to as the "spaghetti swirl" (#482) is probably from the same manufacturer as the Wire Pull. These have been found with groups of Wire Pulls. They have a transparent colored base with opaque swirls or opaque base with transparent swirls. Their value is about the same as Wire Pulls, but varies widely depending on the coloring and the intricacy of the swirling.

Another type of machine made marble known to have been manufactured in Europe are a small group of corkscrew-style marbles (#483) that were made in Czechoslovakia. This small group was found in Europe, and were supposedly manufactured in the 1930s. There were two different types found. One is a corkscrew type that is transparent clear on one side and transparent vaseline yellow on the other. The other is a corkscrew consisting of tiny pieces of colored glass (like Guinea flecks) in transparent clear. Both types were only found in 5/8" size. Only one has been re-sold, that I am aware of, and it was sold for $250.

No doubt additional European marbles will continue to surface as the hobby develops outside of the United States.

#480: Foreign Sparkler

#481: European Wire Pull

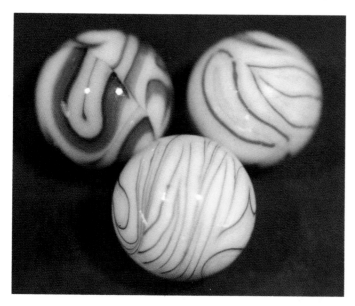

#482: Spaghetti Swirl

133

#483: Czechoslovakia marbles

CAT'S-EYES

Virtually every manufacturer, since the late 1940s, has made cat's-eye marbles. The majority of cat's-eye marbles that you will find are foreign-made. Almost all of those have little value. Many American-made cat's-eyes are beginning to have collector value, with some cat's-eyes selling for $20 or more.

The first American cat's-eyes were manufactured by Peltier Glass Company. This is the Peltier Banana (#297). Bananas are opaque single vane cat's-eyes with occasionally slight ridges in transparent clear glass. They are valued at about $0.50 to $1.00 each (5/8"). The next American manufacturer of cat's-eyes appears to have been Master Glass Company. These are three-vane translucent cat's-eyes in transparent clear glass (#484). They are valued at $0.10 to $0.25 each (5/8"). Another early cat's-eye is the Marble King St. Mary's (#485). This is a four vane cat's-eye with one vane plane in one color and the other vane plane in another color. These have been found in sizes ranging from 5/8" to 1". The value of these was extremely volatile at the time this was written, with values anywhere between $0.10 and $50.00, depending on colors and size.

Cat's-eyes were also made by Vitro Agate (four vane and cage style) (#335), Gladding-Vitro (cage style) (#334), and a number of later manufacturers (#486). American cat's-eyes of later manufacturers have a value of about $0.05 (5/8") to collectors.

Foreign cat's-eyes (#487) were, and continue to be, made in Mexico and the Far East. Most of these are single color four vane, or three color six vane. The glass of many foreign cat's-eyes has a light bottle green tint to it. These do not have much collectible value.

The nine cage cat's-eye (#488) has become very collectible recently. There are three colored sets of three subsurface cage strands in transparent clear glass. These have only been found in about the 5/8" size and are valued from $10 to $35, depending on the colors and quality of design.

American cat's-eyes in colored glass, or cat's-eyes with aventurine or "oxblood" stripes have values that are multiples of those quoted above.

There is still much research that needs to be done into cat's-eye marbles, but some of these are beginning to become quite collectible, something that many collectors would have laughed at a few years ago.

#484: Master Glass Company Cat's-eye

#485: Marble King Inc. St. Mary's Cat's-eye

#486: American Cat's-eyes

#487: Foreign Cat's-eyes

MISCELLANEOUS MACHINE-MADE MARBLES

There are a number of other valuable machine-made marbles that you may run into during your searches.

Marbles with metallic stripes (#342, #343) have been made by several manufacturers, including Alley Agate and Champion Agate. Usually, they have a silvery stripe on the colored swirl of a common swirl marble. Occasionally, you will find a silver stripe on a clearie or a copper colored stripe on a swirl. These are valued in the $7.50 to $20.00 range, depending on the colors in the marble and the width and amount of metallic.

Marbles with aventurine (#344, #345) in them have become popular. Values for marbles with aventurine are listed under each company. The aventurine is actually finely ground metal flecks mixed in with the glass or a component of the glass that crystallized. Aventurine is sometimes found in the black ribbons and patches on Peltier National Line Rainbos and Peerless Patches. It has also been found in common swirls with green swirls on white. It is not known who made these. Those are valued in the $15-$20 range for Mint examples. Aventurine has also been found in some Vitro Agate ribboned marbles. These always have an opaque white base with at least one green ribbon. The 5/8" size is valued around $1. Also, some Vitro Agate four-vane cat's-eyes have been found with aventurine in them. The vanes are usually green and these usually have a lot of "fire" in them. They are valued in the $5-$10 range in Mint condition. Also, on occasion, Marble King Rainbos will contain some large aventurine flakes. A 5/8" Marble King Watermelon with aventurine flakes was sold in a Block's Box absentee auction for $1,050 in early 1997.

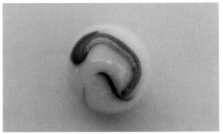

#342: Metallic stripe

#345: Aventurine patch

#343: Metallic stripe

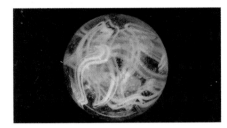

#346: Wire pull ("old")

#344: Aventurine swirl

#347: Wire pull ("new")

COMMON MACHINE-MADE MARBLES

There are literally millions of machine-made marbles in existence. It has been reported that some companies were able to produce several boxcar loads of marbles a day. Most of these were game marbles (opaques), cat's-eyes, swirls and patches.

Almost every machine-made marble produced after 1950 has little or no value to most collectors. There are two reasons for this. First, they were produced in such quantity, that there is an abundant supply of them. Second, the colors are generally dull and the patterns are somewhat non-descript, so they have no eye appeal.

The lack of color and pattern is not an accident. As the toy marble market matured, it was imperative for a manufacturer to cut costs as low as possible in order to compete. The way to do this was to eliminate the expensive materials that it took to produce bright colors and eliminate the inefficient machinery that it took to produce interesting patterns.

Over ninety percent of the machine-made marbles that you run across will not match any of the marbles described above. This does not mean that they are not collectible. There is an almost endless variation of colors and design. Some collectors enjoy putting together collections of these marbles in odd colors and designs, specifically because they are shunned by the majority of collectors. The lack of demand means that this remainder or bulk tends to be valued at a penny to five or ten cents apiece.

Do not toss these marbles aside, just because they have low value. There are many young children who still enjoy playing with marbles and who are not interested in their value. Consider "recycling" your marbles with a local Cub Scout troop (they can get an achievement pin for learning to play marbles) or at a local school. The looks on the kids' faces when you give them your bulk marbles is worth a thousand times more than the marbles you are giving away.

MARBLES IN ORIGINAL PACKAGING

One of the hottest areas of recent interest in marble collecting has been marbles in their original packaging. This is usually limited to machine-made marbles, however, you can find some handmade and non-glass marbles in their original packaging too.

Original packaging serves a very important purpose in the research of marble history. Almost all handmade marbles were sold in bulk, out of bins or large crates. This makes it almost impossible to construct a history of handmade marble manufacturing, or even to identify the country of origin of almost all handmade marbles. Machine-made marbles, on the other hand, were almost always sold in some sort of packaging. This is as much a reflection on the American predilection with marketing as it is on the distribution requirements of the marble manufacturers. As a result, almost every single type of machine-made marble exists in some form of original packaging, making the task of identifying machine-made marbles by manufacturer and date of manufacture fairly easy.

Original packaging can take a number of different forms. These include cardboard boxes, muslin bags, tin boxes, net or mesh bags, cellophane bags, polyvinyl bags and blister cards.

The value of an original package of marbles is determined by a number of factors, including rarity of the package, condition of the package, condition of non-marble items in the package, rarity of the marbles and condition of the marbles. Many types of marbles that are not valuable individually are very valuable when part of a package. This is because the packaging itself is very rare. Many marbles were distributed to retailers in bulk packaging. This bulk packaging (stock boxes, cartons, etc.) can also very rare.

The condition of the packaging itself is the second most important determinant of value (after rarity of the package). Rips, tears, burst corners, water stains, rusting, tape tears, or scribbling on the package by an earlier owner, all depreciate the value of the packaging.

In many cases, packaging came with ancillary items: Kneepads, marble game instructions, contest cards. These items can greatly enhance the value of the original packaging.

Handmade or non-glass marbles in their original packages are fairly rare. These usually are cardboard boxes of sulphides (#348), swirls, benningtons, clays (#349, #350, #352, #353) or chinas, or muslin bags of clays (#350). Original packaging containing machine-made marbles are much more plentiful.

The most difficult to find are cardboard boxes from the M.F. Christensen & Son Company. These are extremely rare and only a handful are known to exist. Any packaging with the M.F. Christensen name on it is extremely valuable. There are some rectangular boxes that can be found which contain slags. These are referred to as "sampler" boxes and are believed to have been part of a salesman sample case (#354). Stock boxes that were shipped to retailers had the name of the company and type of marble stamped on the top (#355) or on an end flap (#356).

Original boxes from the Christensen Agate Company are also very rare, although not nearly as rare as M.F. Christensen. Some of the boxes are typical retailer stock boxes with the name of the company and the marble type stamped on them (#357). Christensen Agate marbles can also be found in boxes from the J.E. Albright Company and M. Gropper & Sons Company (#358). Christensen Agate also used the smaller square stock boxes. These were imprinted with the company name and type of marble on the cover. The boxes typically held 25 marbles (#359, #360). Any packaging from the Christensen Agate Company is very valuable.

Original boxes from the Peltier Glass Company are surprisingly difficult to find, given the fact that the company produced so many marbles for so long. The M.Gropper No. 28 Lucky Boy box (#361) is probably the most common. These originally contained Peltier marbles, usually tri-color National Line Rainbos. Peltier also used retailer stock boxes with only the name of the company and the type of the marble stamped on them. Later packaging was more ornate and printed, rather than stamped. Peltier sold marbles in several different 100-count cubes (#362), as well as 5-count and 10-count lithographed cutout boxes. These are relatively easy to find. Peltier also sold a number of different gift sets, all of which are very difficult to find today (#363, #364). In addition to the gift boxes, the rarest Peltier packages are the four different-size boxes that Picture Marbles or comics came in. These include a small red box that held five comics (#365), a larger red or yellow rectangular box that held a complete set of twelve comics, a small square box that held twenty comics (#366) and an extremely rare rectangular box that held twenty comics. This last box is almost impossible to locate. Later Peltier packaging includes net bags (#367) and polyvinyl bags. Recently, a Chinko-Checko-Marblo box was found which was printed with the Peltier name, rather than Berry Pink, Inc.

Packaging from the Master Marble Company, Master Glass Company, and Vitro Agate Company are easier to find. Master Marble used gift sets (#368, #369), as well as retailer stock boxes (#370). They also used some mesh bags. Master Glass used boxes, mesh bags and polyvinyl bags. Vitro Agate company used the full range of packaging. The earliest and rarest packaging is retailer stock boxes (#371) and cardboard marble sets (#372). Vitro was one of the few companies to use cellophane for its bags. They also produced a wide range of mesh bags (#373) and polyvinyl bags (#374). Gladding-Vitro used polyvinyl bags, as did the later incarnations of the Vitro Agate Company.

Akro Agate Company was the most prolific user of boxes and tins. One of the most difficult Akro Agate boxes to find is the Akro Agate Salesman's Sample case (#375). This was the labeled case of marbles carried around by salesmen as they made their calls. Less than ten were known to exist when the first edition of this book went to press. Since then, a number have surfaced. There are also other Akro Agate sampler boxes that can be found (#376).

Akro Agate, as did other companies, used a variety of stock boxes to ship their marbles to retailers for display and sale. The earliest retailer stock boxes have the marble type and size stenciled on the cover with a small logo printed in the corner (#377). Other stock boxes had a label with the company logo pasted on the top and a label with the type of marbles pasted on an end flap (#378). These are still early Akro boxes and are rare. Later stock boxes had the company logo printed on the top and the marble type printed on the end flap (#379). Akro Agate also used a number of the printed square display boxes (#380, #381). Unique to Akro Agate was a series of cardboard sleeve display boxes (#382) and two different sizes of gift tins (#383, #384). Akro Agate also used several different types of cardboard gift boxes (#385, #386, #387, #388). The most collectible gift boxes are the Popeye boxes (#389, #390). Another rare box, unique to Akro Agate, was the bubble gum box (#391). These are very difficult to find. Akro Agate also produced several types of Chinese Checker boxed sets (#392), as did many other companies and distributors (#402). They also used mesh bags late in the company's history (#393). These are more difficult to find than Akro boxes. Other companies that used mesh bags were Alox Manufacturing (#394), Ravenswood Novelty and Vitro Agate.

Plastic bags of marbles began to proliferate in the late 1940s and early 1950s. The first bags were a cellophane material, but this material cracked and tore easily. This was quickly replaced by polyvinyl, which is more rubbery and forgiving. In the mid-1980s, plastic mesh bags began to appear. Virtually every manufacturer since 1950 has sold marbles in plastic poly bags (#401). Packaging from Marble King and other later manufacturers are almost all polyvinyl bags (#396, #397) and blister packs (#400). Berry Pink also produced a few cardboard gift boxes (#395) early in its history, and used mesh bags (#398, #399) before polyvinyl bags.

On the next few pages are pictures of various examples of packaging with their estimated values. This is by no means an exhaustive list as new items are constantly being rediscovered. This topic, as well as marble-related items (medals, games, advertising), is covered in much greater detail in the book, *Marble Mania*™.

#348: Original box of twelve sulphides. Circa 1900. (marbles are 7/8"). (German). $3,000-$4,500.

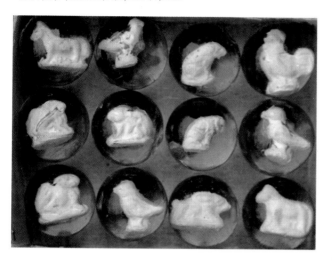

#349: Original box of dyed clays. Circa 1920. (German). $100-$150.

#350: Original muslin bag of dyed clays. J.E. Albright Company. Circa 1920. $200-$400.

#352: Original jobber boxes of clays. Circa 1920. Front view. $100-$150 each.

#351: Original box of dyed clays. J.E. Albright Company label pasted on a Christensen Agate Company box. Circa 1925. $300-$500.

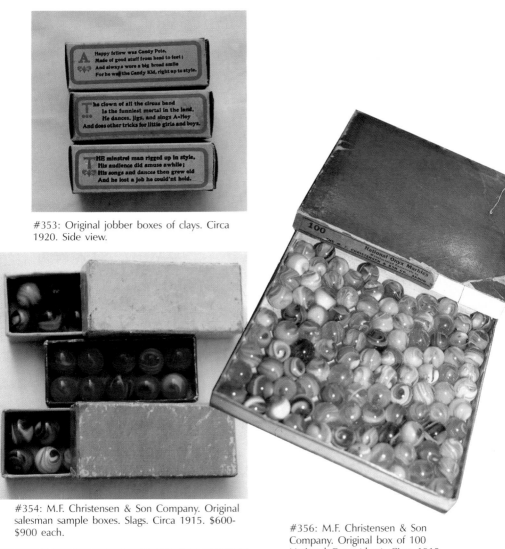

#353: Original jobber boxes of clays. Circa 1920. Side view.

#354: M.F. Christensen & Son Company. Original salesman sample boxes. Slags. Circa 1915. $600-$900 each.

#356: M.F. Christensen & Son Company. Original box of 100 National Onyx (slags). Circa 1915. $5000-$7500 (if Mint).

#355: M.F. Christensen & Son Company. Original box of 12 No. 2 Persion Turquoise. Circa 1915. $2500-$4000.

143

#357: Christensen Agate Company. Original box of 50 No. 2 slags. Circa 1930. $2,250-$3,500.

#358: Christensen Agate Company. Original box of 100 No. 0 World's Best Guineas. (no marbles). Circa 1930. $450-$700 (without marbles).

#359: Christensen Agate Company. Original box of 25 No. 1 cobras. (American Agates box). ("C" stands for Clearies). Circa 1930. $18,000-$25,000.

#360: Christensen Agate Company. Original box of 25 No. 1 World's Best Moons. Circa 1930. $4,000-$7,000.

#361: Peltier Glass Company. No. 28 Lucky Boy box with tri-color National Line Rainbos. Circa 1930. $2,250-$4,000 (box empty is $200-$300).

#362: Peltier Glass Company. Big Value Marble Assortment. Circa 1935. $150-$250.

#363: Peltier Glass Company. No. 224 National Marble (Gift) Set. Circa 1930. $2,500-$4,000.

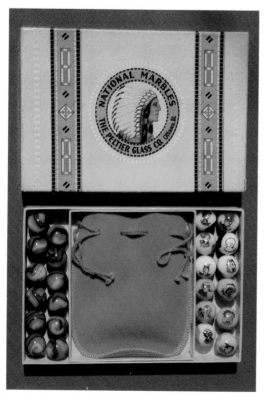

#364: Peltier Glass Company. National Marble (indian head) (gift set). Circa 1930. $5,000-$8,000.

#367: Peltier Glass Company. Champion Jr. mesh bag. Circa 1940. $60-$125.

#365: Peltier Glass Company. 5 count Picture Marble box. Circa 1930. $600-$2,500 (depending on comic characters on marbles).

#368: Master Marble Company. Gift Set. Circa 1935. $400-$800.

#366: Peltier Glass Company. 20 count Picture Marble box. Circa 1930. $2,000-$6,000(depending on comic characters on marbles).

#369: Master Marble Company. Game Set. Circa 1935. $250-$400.

#370: Master Marble Company. Retailer stock box of clearies. Circa 1935. $250-$500.

#371: Vitro Agate Company. Box of 100 No. 1 Tri-color Patch. Circa 1940. $500-$750.

#372: Vitro Agate Company. Box of 60 No. 0 Opaque. Circa 1940. $45-$90.

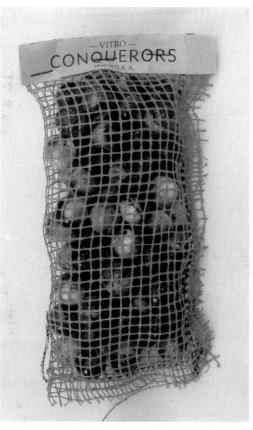

#373: Vitro Agate Company. Conquerors in mesh bag. Circa 1945. $30-$60.

#374: Vitro Agate Company. Bottle-hanging advertising polyvinyl bag. Circa 1950. $20-$35.

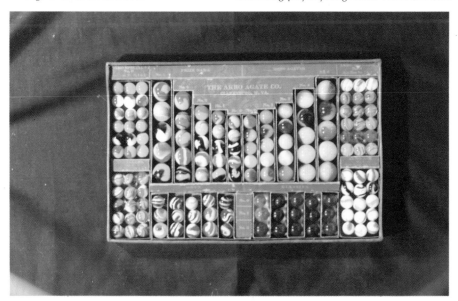

#375: Akro Agate Company. Original Salesman's Sample Case. Circa 1930. $7,500-$12,500.

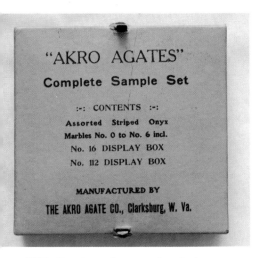

#376: Akro Agate Company. Sampler box (empty). Circa 1935. $500-$800.

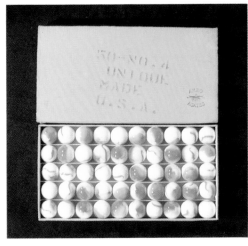

#377: Akro Agate Company. Original box of 50 No. 4 Uniques. Circa 1925. $1,500-$2,500.

#378: Akro Agate Company. Retailer stock box of 100 No. 2 Prize Names. Circa 1930. $650-$1,000.

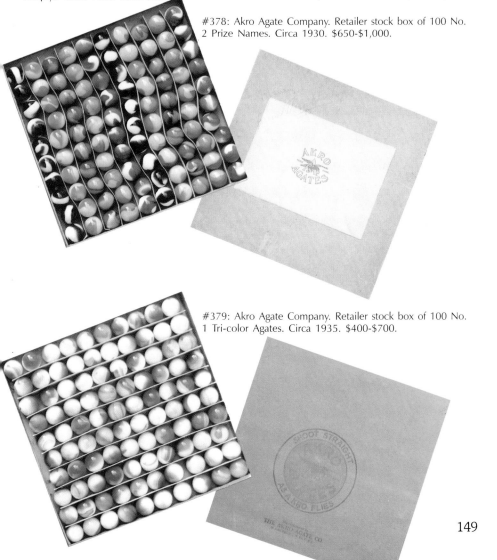

#379: Akro Agate Company. Retailer stock box of 100 No. 1 Tri-color Agates. Circa 1935. $400-$700.

#380: Akro Agate Company. Original box of 25 No. 0 (brown) Flinties. Circa 1930. $750-$1000.

#381: Akro Agate Company. Original box of 25 No. 1 Cardinal Red. Circa 1930. $600-$900. (Box of No. 0's is $300-$500)

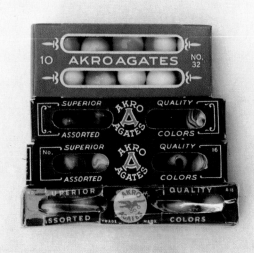

#382: Akro Agate Company. Assorted cardboard sleeves. Circa 1928-1935. (Top is $125-$200, bottom three are $90-$150).

#383: Akro Agate Company. No. 150 tin (top of lid). Circa 1935. $125-$250 (empty with trays), $500-$900 (full, depending on marbles).

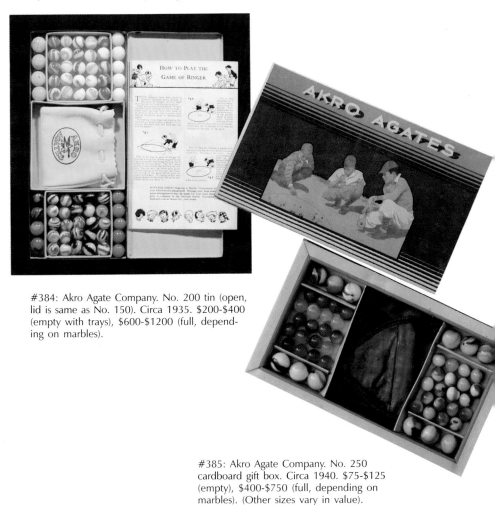

#384: Akro Agate Company. No. 200 tin (open, lid is same as No. 150). Circa 1935. $200-$400 (empty with trays), $600-$1200 (full, depending on marbles).

#385: Akro Agate Company. No. 250 cardboard gift box. Circa 1940. $75-$125 (empty), $400-$750 (full, depending on marbles). (Other sizes vary in value).

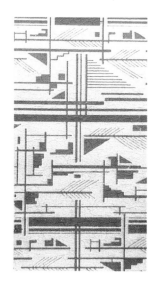

#386: Akro Agate Company. No. 250 Gift Set (embossed foil lid). Circa 1935. $800-$1,400 (with Moss Agates).

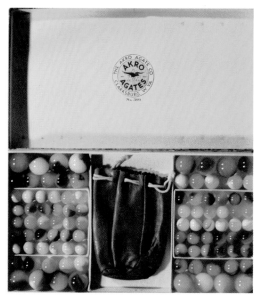

#387: Akro Agate Company. No. 300 Gift Set (embossed foil lid). Circa 1935. $1,250-$2,500 (with Moss Agates).

#388: Master Marble Company. Stained glass gift box. Circa 1935. $750-$1200.

152

#389: Akro Agate Company. Popeye box (red, No. 116). Circa 1930. $900-$1500.

#390: Akro Agate Company. Popeye box (red, unnumbered, larger size prototype). (only two known to exist). Circa 1930. $6,000-$10,000.

#391: Akro Agate Company. Retailer bubble gum box. Circa 1940. $5,000-$9,000.

#392: Akro Agate Company. Original box of 60 No. 0 Chinese Checkers. Circa 1940. (red is $45-75, tan is $20-$35).

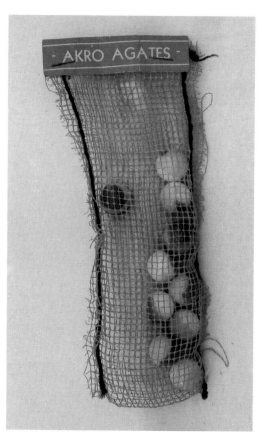

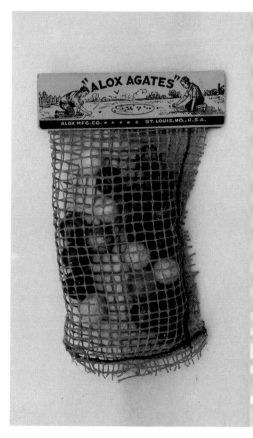

#393: Akro Agate Company. Original mesh bag. Circa 1945. $125-$250.

#394: Alox Manufacturing Company. Alox Agates in mesh bag. Circa 1945. $75-$125.

#395: Berry Pink, Inc. Champion marbles gift box. Circa 1930. $500-$900.

#396: Marble King. Inc. Rainbows in polyvinyl bag (30 count). Circa 1950. $25-$50.

#398: Marble King. Inc. Peltier Glass Company marbles in mesh bag. Circa 1945. $40-$75.

#397: Marble King. Inc. Rainbows in polyvinyl bag (100 count). Circa 1950. $60-$100.

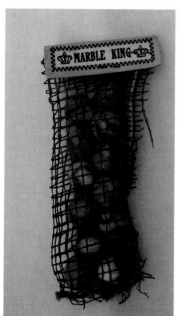

#399: Marble King. Inc. Peltier Glass Company marbles in mesh advertising bag. Circa 1945. $40-$75.

#401: C.E. Bogard & Sons Inc. Catseyes in polyvinyl bag. Circa 1975. $15-$25.

#402: L.G. Ballard Manufacturing Company. Original jobber box of opaques. Circa 1940. $50-$80.

#403: Original jobber box. Circa 1945. $5-$20 (depending on box and marbles).

#400: Marble King. Inc. Blister pack. Circa 1970. $5-$7.50.

CONTEMPORARY HANDMADE GLASS MARBLES

Over the past ten years, there has been an explosion of contemporary glass workers who are handcrafting works of art. What better way for them to show off their skill, artistic talents and craftsmanship than to make orbs and spheres to showcase their art.

Some of these craftsmen produce similar designs each year, while others are constantly creating new forms, techniques and designs. There are a multitude of contemporary marble makers. This section contains a sampling of the work of some of these artists.

The book, *Marble Mania*™, has an expanded section on contemporary marbles. The book *Contemporary Handmade Marbles and Related Art Glass* was published in 2001.

The prices shown in this section are current retail prices from either the craftsmen themselves or from the secondary market.

The artists illustrated here are those who had contacted the Society prior to publication of the first edition of this book. Additional marble makers are illustrated in the books mentioned above. All of the artists show here create their marbles utilizing kiln-techniques, not lampworking (bead-making). Marbles made using lampworking techniques are valued significantly lower than those shown here.

Geoffrey Beetem - Ohio (#404, #405)
Geoffrey Beetem Designs
Born 1951, Philadelphia PA
Produces clambroths, "tidal pools", ribbon cores
and ribbon cores with lutz. Valued $35 to $4000.

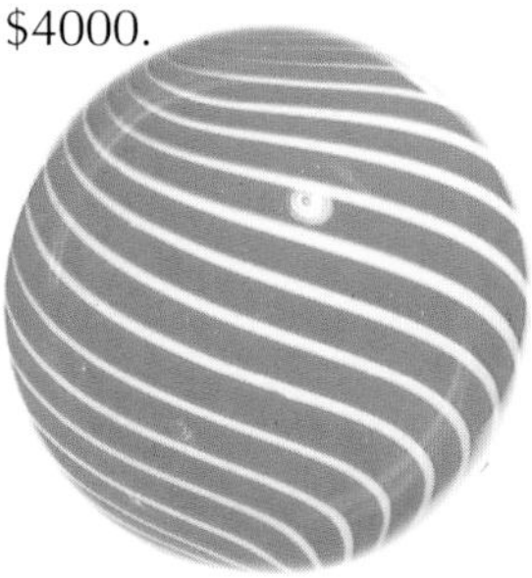

#404: Geoffrey Beetem. Clambroth.

#405: Geoffrey Beetem. Ribbon core swirl with lutz.

Harry Bessett - Vermont (#406, #407)
Born 1957
Produces swirls, and a marble with raised figures (letters, numbers, animals, planes, stars, etc.). Valued $25 to $900.

#406: Harry Bessett. Latticinio core swirl.

#407: Harry Bessett. Ribbon core swirl.

Harry & Kathleen Boyer - Michigan (#408, #409)
Boyer Glassworks
Born 1950, Ohio (Harry) & 1951, New Jersey (Kathleen)
Produced paperweight type with flowers or millefiori and swirls and end of day onion-skins with lutz. Valued $40 to $250.

#408: Harry & Kathleen Boyer. Flower.

#409: Harry & Kathleen Boyer. End of day onionskin with aventurine.

William Burchfield- Massachusetts (#410, #411)
Cape Cod Glass
Produced swirls, clambroths, end of day and "crown filligree." Valued $50- $250.

#410: William Burchfield. Millefiori.

#411: William Burchfield. Crown filigree.

Buddy Buttler - Indiana (#412, #413)
Prestige Art Glass Company
Born 1953
Produced sulphides and swirls. Valued $50 to $100.

#412: Buddy Buttler. Swirl.

#413: Buddy Buttler. Sulphide.

Nina Paladino Caron - California (#414, #415)
(see also Michael Hansen)
California Glass Studios
Born 1949, Sacramento, California
Produces "swirls." Valued $45 to $100.

#414: Nina Paladino Caron & Michael Hansen.
Coiled core swirl.

#415: Nina Paladino Caron & Michael
Hansen. Coiled core swirl.

Christopher Constantin - Massachu-
setts (#416, #417)
(see also Kathy Young)
North River Glass
Born 1957, Louisiana
Produced end of day with hearts.
Valued $75 to $200.

#417: Christopher Constantin & Kathy
Young. End of day.

#416: Christopher
Constantin & Kathy Young.
End of day.

159

James Cooprider - California (#418, #419)
Produced swirls with lutz, corkscrews and other types. Valued $50 to $100.

Terry Crider (#420, #421)

#418: James Cooprider. Ribbon core swirl with lutz.

#419: James Cooprider. Ribbon core swirl.

Produces swirls with mica, clambroths with mica and end of days with lutz. Valued $50 to $150.

Robert Dane - Massachusetts (#422, #423)

#420: Terry Crider. Banded swirl with mica.

#421: Terry Crider. Clambroth.

Born 1953
Produced swirls, end of days, "latticinio spheres", "colossal spheres" and "combination marbles." Valued $40 to $700.

#422: Robert Dane. Banded swirl.

#423: Robert Dane. End of day.

Jim Davis - Indiana (#424, #425)
Born 1931, West Virginia
Produced sulphides, swirls, end of days. Valued $40 to $150.

#424: Jim Davis. End of day.

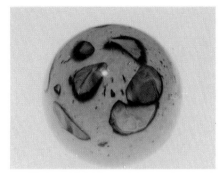

#425: Jim Davis. End of day.

Shanti Devi - California (#426, #427)
Kaimana Glass
Born 1953, Michigan
Produced 'dichoric starbles' with futuristic metallic shapes in glass and freeform swirls.
Valued $100 to $300.

#426: Shanti Devi. Starble.

#427: Shanti Devi. Starble.

James Dunlavy - Indiana (#428, #429)
Dunlavy Glass
Born 1932, West Virginia
Produced swirls and onionskins. Valued $50 to $150.

#428: James Dunlavy. End of day.

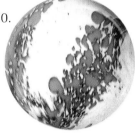

#429: James Dunlavy. End of day.

Jody Fine - California (#430, #431)
J. Fine Glass
Born 1952
Produces swirls and "Murrini" marbles. Valued $10 to $100.

#430: Jody Fine. Latticinio core swirl.

#431: Jody Fine. Latticinio core swirl.

Dudley Giberson - New Hampshire (#432, #433)
Giberson Glass
Born 1942, Illinois
Produced swirls with lutz. Valued $75 to $350.

#432: Dudley Giberson. Ribbon core swirl.

#433: Dudley Giberson. Ribbon core swirl with lutz.

Charles Gibson - West Virginia (#434, #435)
Gibson Glass Company
Born 1933
Produces sulphides, swirls, "snakeskins" and end of days. Valued $15 to $75.

#434: Charles Gibson. Sulphide.

162

#435: Charles Gibson. End of day.

David Gruenig - Vermont (#436, #437)
Gruening Glass Works
Born 1939
Produced slags and end of days. Valued $50 to $150.

#436: David Gruenig. End of day.

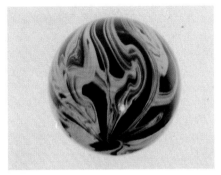

#437: David Gruenig. End of day.

Michael Hansen - California (#414, #415)
(see also Nina Paladino Caron)
California Art Glass
Born 1947, Oceanside, California
Produces "swirls." Valued $45 to $100.

#439: Fritz Lauenstein.
Ribbon core swirl.

Fritz Lauenstein - Massachusetts (#438, #439)
Fritz Glass
Born 1959, Illinois
Produces swirls. Valued $25 to $100.

Robert Lichtman - Connecticut (#440, #441)
Sugar Hollow Glass Studio
Born 1958 - Illinois
[Currently only producing marbles for kaleidescope makers]
Produced swirls and end of days. Valued $50 to $150.

#438: Fritz Lauenstein.
Ribbon core swirl.

15040: Robert Lichtman. End of day.

#441: Robert Lichtman. Ribbon core swirl.

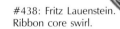

Brian Lonsway - Ohio (#442, #443)
Produced swirls. Valued $50 to $200.

#442: Brian Lonsway. Banded swirl. #443: Brian Lonsway. End of day.

Steven Maslach - California (#444, #445)
Maslach Art Glass
Born 1950, California
Produces swirls, end of days, clambroths. Valued $10 to $130.

#444: Steve Maslach. Latticinio core swirl. #445: Steve Maslach. Ribbon core swirl.

Mark Matthews - Ohio (#446, #447)
Matthews Art Glass
Born 1954, Ohio
Produces swirls, end of day, clambroths, lutzes, Graal, and groupings . Valued $35 to
$60,000.

#446: Mark Matthews. Joseph's Coat swirl. #447: Mark Matthews. Ribbon core swirl.

D. Grant Maul - Michigan (#448, #449)
Hope Glass Works
Produced swirls. Valued $50 to $150.

#448: D. Grant Maul.
End of day.

#449: D. Grant Maul. Latticinio core swirl.

Michael Max - Washington (#450, #451)
Produced swirls. Valued $50 to $150.

#450: Michael Max. Ribbon core swirl.

#451: Michael Max. Swirl.

Anthony Parker - Oregon (#452, #453)
Fulton Parker Glass Company
Born 1945, Oregon
Produces paperweight, freeform swirl, floral and dichroic numbers.
Valued $30 to $150.

#452: Anthony Parker. Paperweight marble.

#453: Anthony Parker. Freeform marble.

Robert Pelletier - Germany (#454, #455)
Produced swirls. Valued $50 to $150.

#454: Robert Pelletier. Banded swirl.

#455: Robert Pelletier. Slag.

Ro and Catherine Purser - Washington (#456, #457)
Noble Effort Design
Born 1949, Alaska (Ro)
Produces millefiori and sulphide. Valued $150 to $750.

#456: Ro and Catherine Purser. Latticinio
core swirl.

#457: Ro and Catherine Purser. Millefiori.

Joe Rice - Indiana (#458, #459)
House of Glass
Born 1950
Produced sulphides, swirls, onionskins. Valued $40 to $1000.

#458: Joe Rice. Sulphide.

#459: Joe Rice. Flower.

David P. Salazar - California (#460, #461)
David P. Salazar Art Glass
Born 1950
Produces intricate paperweight marbles. Valued $35 to $350.

#460: David Salazar. Aquarium.

#461: David Salazar. Butterfly.

Josiah Simpson - Massachusetts (#462, #463)
Born 1949
Produces "planets." Valued $40 to $500.

#462: Josiah Simpson. Planet.

#463: Josiah Simpson. Planet.

Russell C. Stankus - Virginia (#464, #465)
Produced swirls. Valued $50 to $150.

#464: Russell Stankus. Joseph's Coat swirl.

#465: Russell Stankus. Paperweight marble.

Joseph St. Clair - Indiana (#466, #467)
St. Clair Glass
Born 1909. Died 1985.
Produced slags and sulphides. Valued $75 to $300.

#466: Joseph St. Clair. Sulphide.

#467: Joseph St. Clair. Slag.

Douglas Sweet - Ohio (#468, #469)
Karuna Glass
Born 1939
Produces "landscapes" and "orbs." Valued $40 to $300.

#468: Douglas Sweet. Orb.

#469: Douglas Sweet. Landscape.

Rolf and Genie Wald - Washington (#470, #471)
Wald Glass
Born 1957, Wilmington, Delaware (Rolf), and 1959, Anaheim, California (Genie)
Produce swirls with lutz, end of days with lutz, "beach balls" with lutz, ribbon lutzes. Valued $20 to $300.

#471: Rolf and Genie Wald. Beach ball with lutz.

#470: Rolf and Genie Wald. End of day with mica.

Jonathan Winfisky - Massachusetts (#472, #473)
Born 1955, Massachusetts.
Produced "coiled", "confetti" and "spiral." Valued $50 to $150.

#473: Jonathan Winifsky. End of day.

#472: Jonathan Winifsky. Ribbon core swirl.

Kathy Young - Massachusetts (#416, #417)
(see also Christopher Constantin)
North River Glass
Born 1954, New Jersey
Produced end of day with hearts. Valued $75 to $200.

Joseph, Bart & Kerry Zimmerman - Indiana (#474, #475)
Zimmerman Art Glass
Born 1923 (Joe, deceased), 1959 (Bart), 1961 (Kerry)
Produced onionskin, swirl, end of day with lutz. Valued $50 to $60.

#474: Joseph, B150. & Kerry Zimmerman. End of day.

#475: Joseph, Bart & Kerry Zimmerman. Mica.

REPRODUCTIONS, FAKES, FANTASIES & REPAIRED MARBLES

As with any collectible today, you should be aware that there are reproductions, fakes, fantasies, reworked, remelted and repaired marbles out there.

Reproduction of marble types is not a new phenomena. In fact, several of the early American marble companies attempted to produce machine-made marbles that reproduced handmade marbles. Sparklers and Sunbursts were an attempt to mimic onionskins; cat's-eyes were an attempt to mimic swirls; Bricks, slags and Akro Carnelian Agates and 'Ades were an attempt to mimic handcut stones. All of these marbles, with the exception of the cat's-eyes perhaps, are highly collectible today.

As modern glass craftsmen began to produce contemporary handmade marbles twenty five years ago, they naturally turned to antique handmade marbles as a guide. The Marble Collectors Society of America has been at the forefront of convincing many contemporary artisans to sign their marbles. This serves a two-fold purpose: A signed marble is not mistaken for an antique, and someday, when the marble does become an antique, the maker can still be recognized for his work. There are only a couple of contemporary artisans who still do not sign their works, but the number is much fewer than even five years ago. Unsigned contemporary handmade marbles can be identified by several features. First, the glass tends to be much clearer than you see in antique marbles. Old glass tends to have at least some tiny air bubbles in it. Contemporary marbles usually do not have tiny air bubbles in them that are not part of the design. Second, contemporary marbles usually have colors that you do not see in antique marbles. The colors tend to be much brighter than old colors. Third, contemporary marbles have a very smooth surface. Antique marbles almost always have ripples and creases running around the circumference of the marble in the glass, no matter how tiny those marks may be. Generally, the surface of contemporary marbles is much smoother and more uniform than antique marbles. Finally, contemporary marbles almost always do not have a pontil or the pontil is fire-polished. Antique marbles always have a pontil, although it may be ground. A modern artisan takes much more time with his marbles than the old craftsmen. Even if the pontils of an old marble were smoothed, it was usually done in a rush.

Peltier Glass Company comics have been reproduced for at least the past fifteen years. The original comics were made by a process that applied and fired a graphite image to the surface of a Peltier Peerless Patch. The marbles were always 19/32" to 11/16" in diameter and the transfers were always black (except for a couple of extremely rare experimentals). The reproductions that I have seen are of several different types. The twelve original comic characters (as well as the Cotes and Tom Mix) have been reproduced on Peltier Peerless Patches. However, the images have either been painted on, silk-screened on or applied as a decal. In all cases, if you rub your finger over the transfer, you can feel that it is on top of the marble surface. You cannot feel the transfer on an original comic because it was fired onto the marble. I have also seen reproduction comics on Marble King or Vitro Agate patch & ribbon marbles. Finally, I have seen reproduction comics on marbles larger than 11/16". There are also some reproduction comic marbles that have transfers of images that were never on the originals. These include Popeye and Jeff (of Mutt and Jeff). Usually, these are multicolor, which the original Peltier comics are not. Also, a firm by the name of Qualatex made a large number of advertising marbles during the 1970s and 1980s. These have a multitude of single color and multicolor images on them. They are not Peltier comics.

The recent explosion of interest in machine-made marbles has produced a new type of glassworker. These glassworkers, and there are only a few at this time, are making marbles that mimic machine-made marbles. They sometimes do this with glass from old marbles or cullet (re-works), and sometimes from new glass (reproductions). These glassworkers have resisted all attempts to convince them to sign their marbles. Some of their new designs are virtually indistinguishable from the original marbles to all but the most advanced collector. Among the marbles that these glassworkers have been reproducing are Leighton transitionals (transitionals with oxblood), rare and hybrid oxbloods, large slags, Christensen Agate Guineas and swirls, and Peltier National Line Rainbos. You must be very careful when buying these types of marbles.

Re-worked marbles are marbles that are made from pieces of original marbles, cullet glass or a combination with new glass. Most of the re-worked marbles that I have seen are re-worked Leighton transitionals, Bricks and oxbloods. These marbles are generally made by a process which melts or layers colors together or on top of one another. Most of these have been ground and polished. This is necessary because the process of making them does not create a smooth surface. Therefore, you can see grinding and polishing marks on each of the marble surfaces, especially if viewed under a 10x lens. Also, the polishing exposes air holes that were laying just beneath the surface. These air holes do not have melted edges, but rather have sharp edges that resulted from the polishing. For those re-worked marbles that have not been ground or polished, the ones that I have seen have short, melted pontils or else have been fire polished. The surface is not completely smooth, but has melted ripples on it. Some early examples had vastly different colors of glass in them or had tiny copper pieces embedded in them. Be very aware of re-worked marbles. None are signed.

Reproduction marbles are contemporary marbles that are made to duplicate as closely as possible the design and coloring of an original marble. I have seen examples of reproduction indians, lutzes, slags, Christensen Agate Guineas and swirls, and Peltier Tri-color National line Rainbos. Reproduction marbles are usually identifiable by a few factors. First, they tend to be the rarer examples. No one is going to take the time to reproduce a $10 or $15 marble, if they can reproduce a $100 or $300 marble with the same effort. Second, they don't look quite right. Trust your intuition. Third, antique handmade marbles always have tiny creases in the glass that resulted from their manufacture. Fourth, look at the pontils and see if they look right. On the other hand, machine-made marbles are a little more difficult. Remember, all machine-made marbles were made by machine (by definition). All reproduction marbles are made by hand. Look very, very closely at the surface. Does it look like it was made by a machine or was it hand-polished or fire polished in some way?

This brings up the topic of repaired marbles (including polished marbles). Polished and buffed marbles are readily identifiable with a little studying. There is no reason to polish or buff a marble, except to remove damage and enhance its collectibility. Handmade marbles should have pontils. Also, handmade marbles always have tiny creases on the surface that are removed by buffing. Look at the chips that remain and see if they have sharp or rounded edges. Rounded edges are usually a sign of buffing. Polished machine-made marbles are a little harder to detect. Almost all machine-made marbles have a very thin layer of surface glass that is removed by buffing. This removal exposes tiny air bubbles on the surface. If you look at these air bubbles and they have polishing grit in them, or the edges are not melted, then the marble has probably been buffed.

Some handmade marbles that have fractures can also be repaired. This is done by re-heating or remelting the marble. This re-heating usually destroys the tiny creases on the surface and also occasionally results in cloudiness in the marble. The process of reforming the marble usually produces concentric tiny creases on the surface that "dance" when the marble is turned in the light.

Fantasies are items that never existed in original form. Examples of these are a recent glut of polyvinyl bags with old looking labels on them. For example, all of the Alox Manufacturing "Army," "Navy" and "Air Force" bags are fantasies, as well as a number of "gasoline station" and "beverage" bags. When looking at polyvinyl bags you should pay close attention to the marbles in them (many polyvinyl bags have modern marbles in them), the cardboard used for the label (does it look and smell old) and the staples used (most old staples are square in profile and will not be shiny).

In conclusion, follow these simple rules of collecting:

1.   Get a money-back guarantee as to the authenticity of anything that you buy. If the seller won't guarantee the authenticity of what they are selling, buy from someone else.

2.   Study your field. There is no substitute for knowledge and hands-on experience. Everyone makes mistakes, but you make less of them if you know what you are looking at.

3.   Keep informed of new finds, rediscoveries and news. Subscribe to one or more of the many newsletters or clubs. Marble Mania® has a quarterly column on new reproductions. The Marble Collecting.com (www.marblecollecting.com) maintains an up-to-date list of reproductions, fakes and fantasies, including images.

4.   Try to attend meets or shows. You can learn more in one weekend of handling items than by reading all of the books in print.

5.   When buying collectibles, only buy items that appeal to you. Don't buy something because you think that it is a good investment or because someone tells you that it is a good buy. Buy it because you like it. If you aren't willing to display it, don't buy it.

6.   Don't ever buy on impulse. Carefully study everything that you are thinking of buying.

7.   Buy the best that you can with your money. Use your precious funds to buy the best SINGLE item, not two or more lesser items. Your collection will be better for it.

GLOSSARY

AGGIE - a shooter made from the mineral, agate.

ALLIES - derived from alley tors; prized shooters made of semiprecious minerals.

ANNEAL - to gradually reduce glass temperature in an oven or Lehr, so as to inhibit cracking in glass.

AVENTURINE - a type of glass containing particles of either copper (goldstone), chromic oxide (green aventurine) or ferric oxide (red aventurine), giving glass a glittering or shimmering appearance.

CANE - a long glass rod constructed of layers of different colors.

CHALKIES - unglazed marbles made from clay, limestone or gypsum.

CHIP - the spot where a piece has broken off the surface of a marble, usually from being hit. Small chips are sometimes called "flakes." A barely visible chip is sometimes called a "pinprick" or "pinpoint."

CLAMBROTH - milk glass marbles in solid color having many thin outer swirl lines of a different color or colors running from pontil to pontil.

CLAY - marbles made of clay which may or may not be colored or glazed.

CLEARIE - clear glass marbles made in a variety of single colors.

CLOUD - an end of day marble where the colored flecks of glass in the marble are not stretched, such that they resemble clouds floating above the core.

COMIC - marbles manufactured by the Peltier Glass Company from 1928 through 1934. They have one of twelve different comic characters stamped and fired onto the marble, such that the transfer is permanent. May also have a transfer of Tom Mix or Cotes Bakery.

COMMIES - playing marbles made out of clay.

CONTEMPORARY GLASS - a marble handmade by a modern craftsman.

CRYSTAL - very clear, colorless glass.

CULLET - pieces of broken glass that are to be added to a batch.

DIAMETER - the length of a straight line through the center of a sphere. The size of a marble is measured by its diameter.

DING - the mark left on the surface of the marble by a small blow. The glass on the area damaged is still intact (unlike a chip). This mark is sometimes called a "moon", "subsurface moon" or "bruise."

DIVIDED CORE - swirl-type glass marble having colored bands in the center running from pontil to pontil.

END-OF-CANE - a handmade marble that was the first (start-of-cane) or final (last-of-cane) one produced from a cane. These are identifiable as marbles where the internal design ends before one of the pontil marks.

END OF DAY - a handmade glass marble that contains small stretched or unstretched flecks of colored glass that do not run continuously unbroken from pontil to pontil.

FRACTURE- an internal stress line caused by a blow to the surface, chemical stress or thermal stress to the glass. This term also refers to a hairline crack in a sulphide figure caused during manufacture.

FREESE IMPROVEMENT - modification made to Akro Agate machinery that eliminated tiny seam at either end of a machine-made marble and made them smoother. Involved off-setting the rollers on the marble-making machine. Named after an

Akro employee and implemented around 1927.

FURNACE - a pot, day tank or continuous tank fabricated for melting glass.

GATHER - a portion of molten glass on a punty, sometimes called a glob.

HANDMADE - marbles that are made without the use of machines. There usually are cut-off marks (pontil marks) on one or both poles of the marble. A handmade glass marble is made by twisting glass off the end of a glass cane or by gathering glass on the end of a metal rod (punty).

IMMIE - a glass marble streaked with color.

INDIAN - handmade marble consisting of dark base glass with colorful bands applied in the surface or on top of it from pontil to pontil.

LATTICINIO - a swirl-type glass marble with thin strands in the center running from pontil to pontil that form a net when the marble was twisted.

LEHR - an annealing furnace or oven.

LUTZ - handmade glass marbles that contain finely ground goldstone.

MACHINE-MADE - a marble that is made by machines. Generally, they are perfectly round and have no pontil marks. These marbles were made after 1900, predominately in the United States.

MANUFACTURING DEFECT - a fold, crease, additional melted glass or open air bubble on the surface of a marble, or a hairline fractures in sulphide figures.

MIBS - the game of marbles, from a shortening of the word marbles.

MICA - mineral silicates that occur in thin sheets and are reflective or silvery in appearance. Coarsely ground flakes of mica are sometimes placed in handmade marbles.

MILKIES - translucent white glassies.

ONIONSKIN - an end of day marble where the colored flecks of glass are stretched, such that the core resembles the skin of an onion.

OPAQUE - a handmade or machine-made marble that is a single color and that is so dark that light does not shine through it.

PEE WEE - a marble that is 1/2" or less in diameter.

PEPPERMINT - a handmade swirl marble that has bands of red, white and blue under the surface.

POLISHED - work which has been done to the surface of a marble to make it more presentable by clearing up cloudiness, surface roughness, scratches or small chips. A polished handmade marble no longer has pontils. A polished machine-made marble is missing the top layer of glass. A handmade marble that has been polished, but that still has its pontils is referred to as "buffed." A machine-made marble that still retains some of its original surface is also referred to by the same name.

PONTIL - a rough mark left on the pole of a marble where it was sheared off a rod or the end of a punty.

PUNTY - a long solid metal rod used to hold a glass object that is being made.

PURIE - a small, brightly colored Clearie.

RIBBON CORE - a handmade swirl with a single or two flat bands in the center running from pontil to pontil.

SHOOTER - the marble used to aim at and strike other marbles in a game. Regulation size is 1/2" to 3/4".

SINGLE GATHER - a marble that was made completely on the end of a punty and not from a cane.

SINGLE PONTIL - a marble with only one pontil, created from either the end of cane or single gathered.

SLAG - a marble made from two different colors of glass that were melted together in the same furnace pot. Due to the differing densities of the glass, they would not melt into a homogeneous color. Handmade slags have pontils. Machine-made slags consist of a colored transparent glass with opaque white swirls.

SOLID CORE - a handmade swirl with a series of bands in the center running from pontil to pontil that are spaced so closely together that no clear space remains between each band.

STEELIE - a marble made out of steel that can be either solid or hollow.

STRIAE - elongated imperfections in glass caused by temperature differences or un-equal density of the materials used. Striae are not fractures.

SULPHIDE - objects made of china clay and supersilicate of potash that are inserted into a transparent glass sphere.

SWIRL - either a handmade marble with bands or strands running continuously unbro-ken from pontil to pontil, or a machine-made marble that is manufactured by injecting one or more colors into a base stream of glass.

TARGET - the marble in a game that was shot at by the shooter. Tournament regula-tions set the size at 5/8".

TAW - derived from alleytor; a prized shooter made of semiprecious stone, usually agate.

TRANSITIONAL - early machine-made marbles that were made partly by hand and partly by machine. Usually the glass was gathered by hand onto a punty and held over the machine. As the molten glass dripped down to the machine, a worker would snip off the proper amount and allow it to fall into the machine to be formed machine. The marble usually has one pontil.

Bibliography

Allen, Shirley "Windy." *The Game of Marbles*. Marble King Inc., 1975.

Barrett, Marilyn. Aggies, *Immies, Shooters and Swirls: The Magical World of Marbles*. Boston: Little, Brown and Company. 1994.

Baumann, Paul. Collecting Antique Marbles. Wallace-Homestead Book Co., 1991.

Block, Mark. *Contemporary Marbles and Related Art Glass*, Schiffer Publishing Ltd., 2000.

Block, Robert. *Marbles Illustrated,* Schiffer Publishing Ltd., 1998.

_____, *Pictorial Price Guide to Marbles*, Schiffer Publishing Ltd. 2002.

Block, Stanley. "Marbles-Playing for Fun and for Keeps." The Encyclopedia of Collectibles-Lalique to Marbles. Time-Life Publications, 1983.

_____, *Marble Mania*, Schiffer Publishing Ltd., 1998.

_____, *Sulphide Marbles*, Schiffer Publishing Ltd., 2000.

_____, *Antique Glass Swirl Marbles*, Schiffer Publishing Ltd., 2001.

_____, *Antique Glass End of Day Marbles*, Schiffer Publishing Ltd., 2002.

Boy Scouts of America. *Cub Scout Sports: Marbles*. 1984.

Carskadden, Jeff, and Richard Gartley. *Chinas: Hand-painted Marbles of the Late 19th Century*. McClain Printing Co., 1990.

Carskadden, Jeff, and Mark Randall. "The Christensen Agate Company, Cambridge, Ohio (1927-1933)." *Muskingum Annals*, Volume 4, 1987.

Castle, Larry, and Marlowe Peterson. *The Guide to Machine-Made Marbles*. Utah Marble Connection, Inc., 1992.

_____, Cat's Eye Marbles, 1998

Degenhart Paperweight & Glass Museum. *Reflection, Guernsey County Glass - 1883-1987*. Self-published, 1989.

Dickson, Paul. "Marbles." *Smithsonian*, April 1988.

Ferretti, Fred. *The Great American Marble Book*. Workman Press, 1983.

Grist, Everett. *Antique & Collectible Marbles*. Collector Books, 1992.

___. Big Book of Marbles. Collector Books, 1994.

___. *Machine-Made and Contemporary Marbles*. 1992.

Hardy, Roger, and Claudia Hardy. *The Complete Line of Akro Agate*. Self-published.

Klutz Press. *The Klutz Book of Marbles*. Klutz Press, 1989.

Ingram, Clara. *The Collectors Encyclopedia of Antique Marbles*. Collector Books, 1972.

Marble Collectors' Society of America. *Marble-Mania*. Quarterly newsletter. Published since 1976.

Marble Collectors' Society of America. *Price Guide*. Self-published, 1989.

Morrison, Mel, and Carl Terrison. *Marbles-Identification and Price Guide*. Self-published, 1968.

Randall, Mark. Marbles as Historical Artifacts. Marble Collectors' Society of America, 1979.

Runyon, Cathy. *Knuckles Down! A Guide to Marble Play*. Right Brain Publishing Co., 1985.

Stanley, Mary Louise. *A Century of Glass Toys*. Forward's Color Productions, date unknown, early 1970s.

Webb, Dennis. *Greenberg's Guide to Marbles*. Greenberg Publishing Co., Second Edition, 1994.